Loyal

Loyal

38 Inspiring Tales of Bravery, Heroism, and the Devotion of Dogs

Rebecca Ascher-Walsh

NATIONAL GEOGRAPHIC

Washington, D.C.

Contents

★ ★ ★ ★ ★ ★

OPPOSITE: *A Red Cross service dog practices rescue techniques for winter conditions.*

Introduction

★ ★ ★ ★ ★ ★

There are dozens of reasons to love dogs, but the paramount reason for my passion emerged while I was writing the prequel to this book, *Devoted: 38 Extraordinary Tales of Love, Loyalty, and Life With Dogs*.

All dog lovers understand that dogs make us our best selves. With their unconditional love, they meet us at a place where we are not judged and can therefore be unguarded. In the privacy of our homes, we're met with chased tails, fetched tennis balls, and endless kisses that inspire us to reclaim our childhood delight in fun. When no one is watching except for the dog, we laugh harder. We hug more. And when we are sad, dogs don't demand explanations or answers. An arm around them in the night, holding them close, will do.

I have known this since childhood—I have never been without a dog by my side. I certainly know it as an adult, volunteering in a high-kill shelter and running the nonprofit Deja Foundation, which offers veterinary and training assistance to dogs rescued from euthanasia in shelters like mine. I understand that just as we can change dogs' lives, they can change ours.

But what I learned as I began to speak with people for *Devoted,* and again while writing this book, is that as powerfully as our love for a dog connects us with the person we are, our collective love of dogs connects us with each other. Across social, economic, and political boundaries, those of us who share this bond are initiated into the most wonderful club. It can happen at the dog park, at work, or simply on the street when we smile at another person walking a sweet companion. Our knowing grins communicate, "How lucky are we?"

That lesson became even more powerful as I wrote *Loyal.* Many of these stories are profoundly emotional. Because these are service or therapy dogs, the needs they met went beyond adding cheer at the end of a long day. Yet, no matter the circumstances, every person I interviewed became elated when talking about their dog, sharing deeply personal experiences from one dog lover to another.

A teacher in Newtown, Connecticut, spoke in detail about the difficult time after the horrific shootings so that we might understand how Drago, a Spinone Italiano, soothed everyone around him. A woman whose calling is comforting traumatized soldiers with Bandit the goofy Great Dane reached out to see which soldiers might want to tell their stories. Suddenly my voice mail was full of people eager to talk about things they didn't share with family members, all in the name of praising Bandit. Even the scientist who spends his life researching threatened and endangered species couldn't contain his enthusiasm for what might otherwise be brutal work if not for his partnership with his cattle dog mix Alli. Her scent-detection skills turn the mission into one of hope.

Equally astonishing: There is not a single person featured in this book who didn't make me laugh—who didn't reconnect with the joy their dog has given them, with the optimism that sometimes only the silliness of a warm muzzle and a silly grin can give. They pay those gifts forward here, telling their stories. The dogs they love, every one of them, are great dogs. And the owners are, without exception, extraordinary people. All are a reminder of how dogs not only help us be our best selves, but also become a better part of the world in which we live. ★

Chaney

A BEST FRIEND ON THE BATTLEFIELD AND BEYOND

Labrador retriever ■ Iowa

★ ★ ★ ★ ★ ★ ★ ★ ★ ★ ★ ★ ★

When he returned from his deployment in Iraq, Marine Matt Hatala thought that the worst possible scenario was being separated from his unit. It never occurred to him that there was something he would dread even more: being reassigned as a handler in the improvised explosive devices (IED) detection dog program.

His first meeting at the South Carolina–based training school with Chaney, the black Labrador retriever with whom he would be paired, did little to convince him otherwise. "I opened the door to the kennel and out came the biggest dog in the group," Hatala remembers. "He was giant; he was rambunctious; he didn't listen; he was pulling me everywhere, and he has this huge head and constantly licks the air like a lizard." Hatala thought to himself, I got the broke dog.

But after seven weeks of training together, Chaney—who had already been deployed as an IED detector in Afghanistan and Iraq with other handlers—earned Hatala's respect. Apparently the marine had earned the dog's, too: "I think he was testing the waters, and once

OPPOSITE: *After serving overseas, Chaney's chief mission is comforting his owner, a fellow veteran.*

*Hatala and Chaney set IED detection
records in Afghanistan.*

he figured out that I was a competent handler, and once I figured out he was a competent dog, we were an amazing pair."

Five months after their first meeting, Chaney and Hatala deployed to Afghanistan. Hatala was struck by the difficulty of being not only responsible for himself in that environment but

also for another living being. "But all the little things I complained about were nothing when you look at the amount of comfort that he brought to us," Hatala says.

At work, the pair was invincible. The group of dogs and handlers that Hatala and Chaney deployed with set a record with the most IED finds in Afghanistan. Chaney was a champion at alerting in addition to being a stellar companion. On missions when the team had to sleep outside, Chaney would lie next to Hatala.

Indeed, the two were by each other's side with few exceptions. "I remember one night being on watch from midnight to 4 a.m., and I got a call from the guy in the command center laughing and saying, 'Dude, get your dog. He's off playing in the puddles,'" Hatala says, adding, "No matter what crazy stuff was going on, having a dog with us was our one normalcy."

Seven months later, Hatala and Chaney landed in Camp Pendleton, California. Hatala had completed his military duty; Chaney was returning to training camp to partner with another handler. As Hatala got off the airplane from Afghanistan and walked over to the truck that would transport his dog back to South Carolina, he says he "cried like a little girl," choking up even now with the memory. "All of us who were putting our dogs on the truck were sobbing."

Soon after, Hatala took a job as a canine trainer at the South Carolina company where Chaney was working with his next marine handler. It was a daily struggle to ignore Chaney in his kennel so the dog wouldn't be confused about who his handler was. "Here's one of my best friends and I couldn't talk to him," Hatala recalls.

Chaney returned to Afghanistan with his new handler; Hatala soon followed, helping British forces stationed in the country work with their IED detection dogs. But he never got over the loss of Chaney. When both were back from Afghanistan once again, Hatala put in an application to adopt him. "He wasn't available yet, but I wanted first dibs," says Hatala, who was living in Iowa at the time. At eight years of age, Chaney wouldn't be deployed again, but Hatala worried about a fire department or a police department recruiting him for his bomb-detection skills. Luckily, neither wanted a dog who could only work for a year or two. Chaney's age was his saving grace.

Two years after they had first parted, Hatala went to pick up his dog. Chaney didn't immediately recognize Hatala, but when Hatala said his name, Chaney "went berserk," Hatala remembers. "Like every one of my military buddies who I haven't seen for years, we just picked up where we left off."

At first, the two had difficulty readjusting to civilian life. Both suffered from nightmares, and Chaney seemed confused that he no longer had a job. Now the two sleep more soundly, and they participate in occasional demonstrations and events, even though Chaney isn't a certified therapy dog. Still, says Hatala, "He's therapeutic for me. Every bad thing I went through, he was there. He's been there for me through everything." ★

Hatala and Chaney enjoy each other's company out of uniform.

Klinger

SETTING THE PACE

German shepherd ▪ California

★ ★ ★ ★ ★ ★ ★ ★ ★ ★ ★ ★

Richard Hunter was used to feeling his way forward at a rapid pace. A marathon runner who also competes in Ironman triathlons, the former marine suffers from the degenerative eye condition retinitis pigmentosa.

A sighted guide would accompany him during races, but it wasn't simple to find companionship for training runs near his home in Northern California. Going solo, he would have to run tentatively, even on routes he had run hundreds of times, and still, he says, "I would be running into things, hitting my face on branches, and wondering if the cars could see me." Hunter's daughter had long encouraged him to get a guide dog, but no organization had yet certified a dog to guide while running. Hunter respectfully abided by that restriction.

Then, at the Boston Marathon in 2014, Hunter met a guy from Colorado who had been running with his guide dog for a long time. It was just the inspiration he needed to turn to another new acquaintance who shared his eye condition, Thomas Panek, and ask, "You're a marathoner, what do you think of running with a guide dog?"

For Panek, who had recently been named CEO of Guiding Eyes for the Blind, a nonprofit

OPPOSITE: *Klinger, one of the first certified running guide dogs, hits the trail for a jog with Hunter.*

organization in New York State, it was an obvious if complicated solution. "It's hard to find a human guide to train with," he says. "And dogs love to run and love to take care of us. But it's a lot of responsibility to guide someone across the busy, noisy streets of Times Square, for example. Now you're raising the bar even higher to ask them to guide you running."

Nevertheless, Panek returned to Guiding Eyes after the marathon and, along with his colleagues, identified a possible candidate: a high-energy German shepherd puppy named Klinger who was being raised in its puppy program. Trained to herd, German shepherds have good pacing, alternating their feet with a long stride that allows them to easily traverse great distances.

At 18 months old, Klinger began training to run. "We have this blooper video where we were trying various things since you can't use a traditional harness," Panek says. By default, Panek became what he calls "the test subject." When he ran with Klinger, Panek experienced the freedom of running without another human being for the first time since he had lost his sight. "It was incredible," he says. "I cried."

In April 2015, Hunter flew across the country to meet Klinger. After a game of fetch with the dog, there was a meeting to introduce Hunter to the key people involved in the project. Panek asked Hunter to share his story and explain why the running guide dog was important to him. "It is very emotional to talk about it and the impact on my family, so I was choking up a bit, and Klinger—even though I had met him only 30 minutes before—got up and laid his head in my lap," Hunter remembers. "He is a dog so filled with empathy and compassion."

After the meeting, Hunter and Klinger went on their first run. With no training in even

THE SEEING EYE The use of guide dogs was pioneered in Potsdam, Germany, where German shepherds were trained to help soldiers blinded during World War I regain their mobility. After a woman living overseas wrote to the *Saturday Evening Post* about it in 1927, the article drew national interest and inspired the founding of the first guide dog training school in the United States.

how to walk with a guide dog, Hunter laughingly describes his experience as being "like a 16-year-old learning to drive clutch for the first time."

Hunter later returned to Guiding Eyes' New York campus to spend three weeks learning the basics of working with Klinger. They were then sent home together. "One of the things my family noticed right away in the airport when I came back with him was that I was moving so fast," Hunter says. "When I traveled with a cane, I was finding obstacles. With a guide dog, you're avoiding them."

As a condition of the program, Klinger and Hunter cannot run farther than six miles together, and Klinger always sets the pace. Whereas human guides aren't always able to show up, Klinger is ready to go, if not always at full speed. "Even if Klinger isn't in the mood that day, the freedom he gives you *so* makes up for it," says Panek of his experience training the dog.

Klinger's success led to Guiding Eyes for the Blind raising a litter of his puppies in hopes they might serve as the next generation of running guides. Hunter is cognizant of his great fortune. "He's an extraordinary dog, not

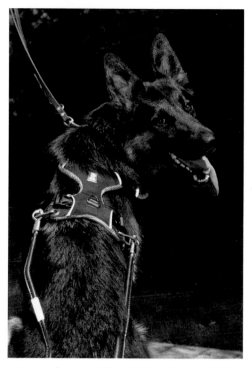

A natural runner, Klinger is Hunter's most reliable training partner and companion yet.

because of me but because everyone put so much work into him. And I have a responsibility to Klinger to do the best I can," he says. "Klinger was born for me. He just didn't know it." ★

Elle

EDUCATING THROUGH KINDNESS

American pit bull terrier ■ North Carolina

★ ★ ★ ★ ★ ★ ★ ★ ★ ★ ★

Elle wouldn't seem the obvious choice for adults trying to overcome a fear of dogs through therapy, or for children learning the rules of canine safety. A sturdy pit bull with cropped ears, Elle can appear ferocious to those who don't know better. But that, says Leah Brewer, who rescued Elle as a puppy, is why Elle's work is all the more important.

Brewer says that people can get "that look" when they see Elle, but she invariably wins them over by the end of every presentation with her calm, patient, and loving nature. "Even people with shaking hands want to come pet her," Brewer says admiringly. "She's changing people's minds about the breed and about dogs, and she's teaching love."

Brewer can relate to people's initial hesitation when approaching Elle. When she and her husband started dating, she remembers, "I was scared of pit bulls because of the media hype around them, but my husband said they were the one and only dog for him, and if I didn't like pit bulls there was no 'us.'" Brewer made a quick decision.

A massage therapist, Brewer introduced Elle to her first therapy work at the retirement home

OPPOSITE: *Charming canine safety advocate Elle dons pearls for a portrait.*

Elementary school students surround Elle, their much respected teacher.

in Roanoke Rapids, North Carolina, where she occasionally works. Then, the pair visited an elementary school where a teacher friend of Brewer's talked about the need for a therapy dog to whom the children could read. Thus began the Tail Wagging Tales program in which Elle works as a reading education assistance dog.

After her work in the school, Brewer designed "P.A.W.S. for Safety," a presentation designed to teach safe dog interaction to students of all ages. The acronym stands for "Pause" before you meet and greet the dog; "Ask" the owner for permission to approach the dog; "Wait" for the dog to approach you; and "Show" the dog respect. "If you go into the dog's space and make that decision for them, that's when a dog will bite," Brewer explains. "But if you let the dog come to you, allowing the dog to make the decision about interacting with you, it's a win-win."

Elle, the winner of a hero dog award from the American Humane Association, is the perfect creature with whom to practice safety, says her owner. In addition to being a good teacher, she thrives on the attention she gets at the P.A.W.S. presentations, where she also performs tricks including high fives and bows. Her only failing: She's been known to fall asleep on the job when children are reading to her at the library. "I'll have to poke her and say, 'Wake up! You're supposed to be listening!'" Brewer laughs.

Otherwise, Elle's enthusiasm for her work is unflagging. "This is what we were meant to do, the two of us," Brewer says. "I want to leave the world a better place than we found it, but Elle wrote her own story, and it's Elle who laid out the path before us. I just hold the leash." ★

Brewster hugs Elle after playtime in Venice Beach's sand and surf.

Echo is more than a guide for John Bramblitt: She's his muse. Bramblitt, who lost his sight due to complications from epilepsy in 2001, thrives on creativity. "Art is a great way to celebrate every good day, and a great way to get through a bad day," says the award-winning painter and author.

Bramblitt started developing his talent at a young age. "I think I could draw before I could walk," he says. He also remembers being sick often and using artwork to cope. But Bramblitt never painted until he became blind—when he became frightened he would forget what color looked like. Now his guide dog, a black Labrador named Echo, is his favorite subject.

Bramblitt paints by feel. He can visualize landscapes, and he is more than familiar with the outlines of Echo's head and body. On the canvas, he makes raised outlines that he then fills, distinguishing colors from one another by their consistency. Bramblitt paints Echo annually, her color on the canvas changes year to year, he explains, because color signifies emotion to him. "The more things we do together, the more complex and brighter her colors become."

Bramblitt and Echo travel often from their home near Denton, Texas, to give workshops or attend art shows. He credits Echo with making it easy to navigate the world of airplanes and hotels; what's more important, however, is Echo allows him to be a better father and husband, thanks to a sense of independence. "She gives me the gift of living my dream every day," he says. "Being blind isn't the end of life, it's just another chapter, and Echo gets that message across better than any person." As do the pictures, which are worth more than a thousand words. ★

Echo

AN ARTIST'S EYES

Labrador retriever ■ Texas

OPPOSITE: *Bramblitt's portraits become more colorful with his growing attachment to Echo.*

Scout

COMMUNITY BUILDER

German wirehaired pointer ■ Idaho

★ ★ ★ ★ ★ ★ ★ ★ ★ ★ ★ ★

His handler, officer Lance Nickerson, lovingly calls Scout "Knucklehead." But to the citizens of Boise, Idaho, Scout is a mascot and community builder who has transformed the pat-down into an art form.

The idea of a therapy dog for the police department came to police chief William Bones while he was visiting his city's weekly farmers market. When he watched a dog there spark interactions among strangers, Bones saw an opportunity for police officers to connect with local residents. "The uniform can be a bit of a barrier," Bones says, but he thought that a dog might be an instant conservation starter, helping with outreach. And it would certainly make work life more enjoyable for his staff. "The first thing people do when they get home from work is pet their dog, so I thought it would fill two great needs," he explains.

Nickerson was selected from a pool of applicants to be the dog's primary handler. He and Scout's secondary handler—a civilian who works in the building—began visiting shelters, forgoing multiple offers of purebred puppies. "We really wanted the opportunity to save an animal who would otherwise lose his or her life and bring some good attention to that cause," Bones says.

OPPOSITE: *Scout's scruffy look draws grins in the Boise Police Department and beyond.*

Fifty potential dogs later, the pair returned from a shelter with Scout—a scruffy, funny-looking mutt by all accounts. "I was thinking some kind of golden-lab mix," recalls Bones. "And when they showed up with Scout, I said, 'Are you kidding me?'" But after a two-week trial stay, everyone knew Scout was the one, a fact Bones laughingly called "strange" given the dog's terrible manners.

Scout was sent to the Idaho Maximum Security Institution, where two inmates spent three months teaching him the skills necessary to be a therapy dog, as well as a few others specific to his line of duty. One of Scout's best tricks: When commanded, he stands against a wall with his paws up and allows Nickerson to perform a search. Another favorite is playing "peeka-boo," when Scout puts his paw over his face. Nickerson admits, "He knows far more tricks than I know how to tell him to do."

Nickerson says his partner Scout has changed his job—and the community's reaction to him. Because his police car says K-9 and has tinted windows, people often assume a biting dog is inside, but when Nickerson lets Scout out of the car, "everyone just loves him to death."

> One of Scout's best tricks: When commanded, he stands against a wall with his paws up and allows Nickerson to perform a search.

WIREHAIR WONDER Bred for the distinctive traits of the pointer, foxhound, and poodle, the German wirehaired pointer evolved as a hunting dog in 19th-century Germany. Its straight, coarse coat is weather resistant so that the dogs work well on land and in water. These dogs need meaningful work, whether it's supporting police or simply retrieving newspapers. Their trademark shaggy beard and eyebrows give them their endearing look, as well as the affectionate nickname "the ugly dog." These resilient pets also have a sillier side that once earned them a gig traveling and performing with the Ringling Brothers circus.

Scout is the center of attention in classrooms, where he champions safety for young students.

Scout, who also visits nursing homes, hospitals, and schools during his off-duty hours, lives with Nickerson and his family, which includes a pit bull and a rabbit. "He puts a smile on everyone's face," says Bones, who now expresses some regret about calling Scout funny-looking when he first arrived. Turns out, the city's goofy rescue "mutt" is, in fact, a purebred German wirehaired pointer whose coat is a defining feature. ★

Bandit

LIFTING SOLDIERS' SPIRITS

European Great Dane ■ Missouri

★ ★ ★ ★ ★ ★ ★ ★ ★ ★ ★ ★ ★ ★

At the United Service Organizations (USO) of Missouri at Fort Leonard Wood, it's not uncommon to see soldiers in uniform sitting on the floor. And beside them, sometimes with his head resting on top of their heads, often with a front leg thrown over their necks in a kind of casual embrace, is a 150-pound Great Dane named Bandit. "The soldiers joke that he's named Bandit because he'll steal your heart," says his owner Kelly Brownfield, center director for the Fort Leonard Wood USO, which provides services to United States troops and their families.

Brownfield adopted Bandit and his brother Duke after they were rescued from a puppy mill. Bandit was born with severe leg deformities that turn one of his legs outward at an angle and have required multiple surgeries, something that Brownfield thinks contributes to his being an "old soul." He was going to be euthanized for illness before she saved his life by taking him home.

The canine brothers began accompanying Brownfield to work when they were still puppies to provide comfort to the soldiers, but it didn't take long to see that Bandit had more to offer than a dog's familiar presence. "Duke is a

OPPOSITE: *The ever popular Bandit's therapy vest is adorned with patches he has earned for his work at the USO.*

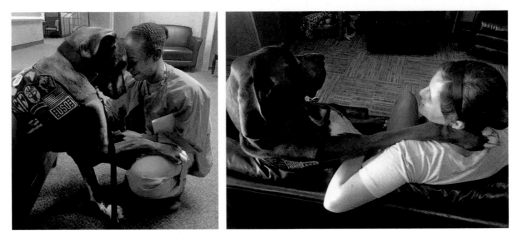

LEFT: *Bandit helps a nurse decompress during a busy day.* RIGHT: *Bandit lends a paw of comfort to a filmmaker who's working on a story about him.*

prankster who wants to play. But from the very beginning, if Bandit saw someone crying in the corner, he would go up to them and either lie down next to them or put his head on their shoulder," Brownfield explains. "We realized that Bandit had some kind of a gift for sensing when something is wrong."

When Bandit turned one year old, Brownfield registered him as a therapy dog. In addition to having free rein over the spacious 18,000-square-foot facility, Bandit and his owner would visit the post's Warrior Transition Unit—now closed—and soldiers on suicide watch and military family members in need of physical care at the Fort Leonard Wood Hospital. People with deformities are especially quick to connect with Bandit, Brownfield says, because of his. "One day we were in the hospital and a little girl was in a wheelchair, and Bandit came up and put his paw on her lap. She grabbed it and turned to her father, this big burly marine, and said, 'See, Dad? I'll be OK. Bandit has a deformity and he's still a hero.' Her dad just started sobbing."

LEFT: *Soldiers soothe Bandit as he recovers from his fifth surgery.* RIGHT: *Poised and dignified in his hat, Bandit gives comic relief to a marine.*

Bandit's daily fans are struggling soldiers whom he seems intuitively to want to palliate. Retired specialist Debra Cruz remembers lying in a hospital after being admitted for chronic unmitigated back pain due to an injury in Iraq that left her with two fractured vertebrae. In addition to physical agony, she anguished over what she knew was the end of her career. Cruz was crying to herself when the curtains parted one day, and there stood Brownfield with this beautiful Great Dane. Tears streamed down Cruz's face.

Cruz remembers that Bandit's height put him right next to her on the bed. "[He] started licking the tears off my cheeks," she recalls. "Immediately I felt calm, and whatever tragedies I was thinking about just went away. All of my thoughts were clear. At that moment, it was just me and Bandit."

Retired staff sergeant Ziva Walters met Bandit when she was assigned to care for the soldiers at the Warrior Transition Unit. "It seems as if he's been thorough as much as our war-torn soldiers who are there," she says.

"You have these service members who don't want to talk about what's happened to them, but you can see their scars. And they look at Bandit with his scars, and it's as if he's saying to them, 'I got you, bro.'" Bandit made it easier for everyone to deal with their daily battles, according to Walters.

Sergeant Donald Walls, who is stationed as a pathologist technician at the hospital, admits that he has been known to put his uniform on when he's not working and head out for a visit with his favorite furry therapist, who is also well known to his children and wife. "He extends himself, which helps especially if you want to get out whatever you're feeling without any judging," Walls says.

Brownfield hears stories of Bandit soothing soldiers every day, and the Great Dane's love has since spread well beyond Missouri. Bandit travels the nation, giving comfort and hope to wounded warriors at Walter Reed National Military Medical Center in Maryland and to families of the fallen at Arlington National Cemetery.

Brownfield marvels, "Someone looked at him and said, 'I swear if you look into his eyes, he has all the answers to all the world's problems.' But I always tell people, 'Just give a dog a chance, and then imagine what he can do.'" ★

> "I swear if you look into his eyes, he has all the answers to all the world's problems."

LOOK OF LOVE When human mothers and children gaze at each other, their brains release a hormone called oxytocin, which has been linked to maternal bonding between many mammal pairs. This trust-building phenomenon may occur across species between humans and canines, as seen in the parental relationships we sometimes develop with our pets. One study shows that the longer a dog gazes at its owner, the higher the levels of oxytocin in the dog's system, and vice versa. The attachment and nurturing behaviors might reinforce each other in a positive feedback loop that deepens the emotional connection and leads to even more interaction.

Bandit and Brownfield share a sweet moment on a sunny day in Washington, D.C.

T rainer Tracy Dulniak had a feeling that the skittish Stevie, whom she pulled off the euthanasia list of a Florida shelter, had the sensitivity of a service dog. He quickly proved her right. "I have epilepsy," Dulniak explains. "And I noticed that with no training, he would come over and butt my hand with his head when I was about to have a seizure." Like her personal service dog, Stevie could sense when something was wrong and alert her before it was too late.

When Monica Alboniga called seeking a service dog for her son Anthony, who has cerebral palsy, Dulniak began training Stevie with then five-year-old Anthony. "There were so many obstacles getting Stevie comfortable with the wheelchair and the sei-zures," Dulniak remem-bers of those first days. "But very shortly they became inseparable."

For Alboniga, Stevie's presence altered their lives immediately. Not only does he alert her to Anthony's seizures, but he also lies across Anthony's body to comfort him and keep him in place before and during an episode. By day, Stevie accompanies Anthony everywhere, from doctor visits to stores; by

night, the dog curls up in bed with Anthony.

But as Anthony prepared for kindergarten, school officials in Broward County, Florida, barred Stevie from accompanying him, demanding that an adult be in control of Stevie at all times—not a requirement of service dogs. Alboniga took them to court and won. "There was no question that Ste-vie is a trained service animal," says the family's attorney, Matthew Dietz. "The judge made the right decision, and this sets major precedence."

Alboniga is grateful that Anthony never has to be without Stevie. "Now I don't worry," she says. "He's completely changed our lives." ★

Stevie

ALL ABOUT A BOY

Pit bull ▪ Florida

OPPOSITE: *The watchful and loving Stevie kisses Anthony's hand while he rests in his mom's lap.*

Riley

Labrador retriever ▪ California

★ ★ ★ ★ ★ ★ ★ ★ ★ ★ ★ ★

It took trainer Kate Davern only three days with Riley to know that it would be impossible to transform the Labrador retriever into a civilized pet for the family who had adopted him. Full of boundless energy, Riley seemed to be an obnoxious dog destined to forever knock children over in his excitement. But Davern also works as a trainer for the National Disaster Search Dog Foundation, and she wondered if what made Riley a less-than-perfect pet could make him a great working dog.

Davern tested him to see if he had what it takes. "He bombed," she recalls cheerfully. "I would ask him to retrieve, and he would run off somewhere else." Undaunted, she began to work on his impulse control, asking him to sit when he would start to race around. Within three weeks, he passed the test with flying colors. Davern then explained to Riley's owners that in their home, he would always be frustrated and getting into trouble. What he needed was a job.

He now has a thrilling one, thanks to the trainers at the Search Dog Foundation who worked with him and then paired him with Eric Gray of the Santa Barbara County Fire Department. Davern jokes that she has bruises for weeks after Riley accidentally runs into her, but

OPPOSITE: *In a rare moment of stillness, Riley sits by his handler, a firefighter who cares for him at work and at home.*

LABRADOR RETRIEVER

❱ **Origin:** Retrievers were bred to retrieve waterfowl for sport hunters and to help fishermen tow in nets. Their sleek bodies are built for swimming and running.

❱ **Temperament:** Gentle and trainable, they are friendly to children and other pets. Loyal Labs excel as guide dogs for the blind and in police work.

❱ **Appearance:** Black Labs were the first, followed by chocolate and then yellow. There are also fawn, fox red, and silver coats.

she says that he's met his match in Gray. "Gray is a muscle man just like Riley," Davern explains. "And like Riley, he is kind and gentle and patient."

Gray says their connection was immediate, despite Riley's bad manners. "You know how you're dancing with a partner and you just fit together? That's what it was like being with Riley." Even so, Gray was terrified of how ill prepared he was to be Riley's handler. Gray remembers telling the dog on their first night together "OK man, it's you and me, and wherever this goes, it's going to be with me."

In addition to regional searches, Riley and Gray have since gone to Japan, after the earthquake-tsunami disaster in 2011, and to Nepal following the earthquake in 2015. Despite grim circumstances, Gray makes it his responsibility to keep Riley energized, which means understanding the art of tug-of-war, one of the rewards for search-and-rescue canines when they alert. It generally takes the dogs 5 to 10 minutes to find someone, and then they get rewarded; but that routine can be hard to maintain in certain situations. "These dogs like to work, but they are like four-year-olds: There has to be fun in there throughout the search, and the day has to end fun for them."

With that in mind, as Gray and Riley toured the empty ruins of their assigned site in Japan, Gray would ask a rescue worker to hide under a mattress every 20 minutes and then send Riley to "find" him. The success recharged Riley's drive to continue looking for survivors and cover as much area as possible.

While Riley hasn't had dramatic finds during his overseas deployments given the devastation on the ground, Gray says Riley's actions are extraordinary when it comes to panicked families. He recounts people standing outside their homes, desperate and fearful that a family member might be inside and asking him to send the dog in to search. "When Riley is done, I am able to turn to them and say, 'No.' What these dogs do more often than not is provide closure that you aren't leaving a loved one behind."

Back in Santa Barbara, Riley accompanies Gray to the fire station and on search-and-rescue missions when required. "Riley is an insurance policy you never want to use," says Gray. "When we get called, something really, really terrible has happened." At home, Riley lives peaceably with Gray, his wife, their young daughter, and a rescued pit bull named Delta. "Riley is an incredible being, and I am so incredibly lucky to have been paired with him," says Gray.

Gray will retire Riley when he finishes his third, three-year-long FEMA certification. "Allowing him to just *be a dog* will be much harder on me than on him," says the firefighter. He dreams that after nine years of a partnership forged by emergencies, the pair will spend their final days together on a beach, running each other to exhaustion. ★

As part of a U.S. rescue team, Gray and Riley search for survivors in northern Japan after the 2011 earthquake and tsunami.

Atlas

A CHAMPION TO CHILDREN

French mastiff ▪ Virginia

★ ★ ★ ★ ★ ★ ★ ★ ★ ★ ★ ★

When canine trainer and behavior expert Kathy Benner started the non-profit Heeling House to focus on animal-assisted therapy for children with special needs, she knew she needed a dog with an unflappable temperament who was also physically solid.

Benner's research led her to Atlas, a French mastiff puppy whom she met when he was four-and-a-half weeks old. "He had been born with a defected tail, so no one else wanted him," she remembers. "Which worked out really well because he was so special. From the beginning, he seemed like an old soul, more interested in being with me than romping with his siblings."

For the next year, Benner took Atlas with her everywhere she went to make sure he was socialized. Shortly after he turned one—the earliest a dog can take the Pet Partners therapy animal evaluation—Atlas became an official therapy dog.

The 120-pound Atlas now works at Children's Therapy Center in Sterling, Virginia. Outfitted with a rope attached to a triangular handle—similar to a water-ski rope—Atlas can pull children down the hallway. Moving slowly, he assists them with balance and walking;

OPPOSITE: *Cherished therapy dog Atlas catches sunlight at a park near the Heeling House office.*

FRENCH MASTIFF

> **Origin:** The French mastiff was once a ferocious breed designed for work as a hunter or fighter. The dogs guarded wealthy masters and baited large game such as bears and bulls.

> **Pedigree:** This breed is also known as Dogue de Bordeaux. The American Kennel Club officially recognized it in 2008.

> **Temperament:** French mastiffs today are gentle giants that make wonderful family pets. They don't require much exercise or grooming, but they are known to drool.

standing still, he allows them to pull themselves up and brace themselves against him.

Angela Henecke, whose son Griffin began working with Atlas when he was four years old, says of her son's transformation, "Griffin didn't really love going to work with his occupational therapist, so one day we decided to try working with Kathy and Atlas. Now, Griffin asks every day if it's Thursday, because that means he gets to see his therapist, which means seeing Atlas." Henecke remembers walking in to see Griffin on a scooter board holding the triangle grip while Atlas pulled him down the hall. "Therapy isn't work for him now," she says. "It's a fun hour he can spend with Atlas."

For Jonathan Ingersoll, Atlas's help is more than physical; memory games like recalling commands for Atlas serve as brain training. "Sometimes when Jonathan is doing something hard, Atlas will just lie next to him and be a friend," says Jonathan's mother, Jennifer.

Atlas is trained to follow touch commands rather than verbal ones so that Brenner's voice doesn't distract the children. He loves his time at the center, according to Brenner, who describes Atlas as "all business." In fact, he gets upset when it's one of the other two therapy dog's turn to work and tries to push them out of the way. "But when it's his turn," Brenner says of Atlas, "he does this happy dance, bouncing and spinning in circles and flying into the car."

As for Atlas's talent, Brenner shrugs, "I'd like to say I'm the best trainer in the world, but somehow, he just knows. He does anything he's asked to do and he's never, ever quit on me. He loves his kids so much." ★

Atlas plays games and assists in exercises that help kids with physical and cognitive development.

When Cindy Ell, founder of the Firefighter Cancer Foundation, invited trainer Janice Wolfe to bring her ridgeback, Wyatt, to demonstrate his cancer-sniffing skills at a meeting of firefighters in New Jersey, she was curious to see how the dog would interact with the crowd. Ell joined the meeting late, but she quickly experienced Wyatt in action.

The ridgeback made a beeline across the room and started poking Ell with his nose. Then, he stood on his hind legs and poked her on the back of the arm before sitting on top of her feet and engaging her in a stare down. "I've got 60 men and Janice staring at me," Ell remembers of the moment. When she asked what the odd behavior meant, Janice explained, "You've all just witnessed a detection."

It turned out that Wyatt had detected a melanoma that doctors had missed. Wolfe, whose own cancer was detected by Wyatt, says that the dog has alerted thousands of unknowing firefighters to illnesses thanks to his instinct and her training.

Wyatt

CANCER DETECTION PRODIGY

Rhodesian ridgeback ▪ New Jersey

Wolfe originally trained Wyatt as a personal service dog to help with her low blood sugar and other health concerns. It became clear that even at a young age Wyatt could detect disease in others based on breath and body scent. "There are things I have taught him but there are some things he just knows," says Wolfe, who trains dogs for the nonprofit organization Merlin's Kids using scent samples.

Wyatt travels the country with Ell and Wolfe vetting firefighters, and the number of people Wyatt has alerted continues to climb. "They all come back and say, 'As a result of Wyatt, I went to the doctor and they found cancer,'" says Ell. Lifesaving acts from one hero to another. ★

OPPOSITE: *Ace disease-detection dog Wyatt and his handler navigate the streets of New York City.*

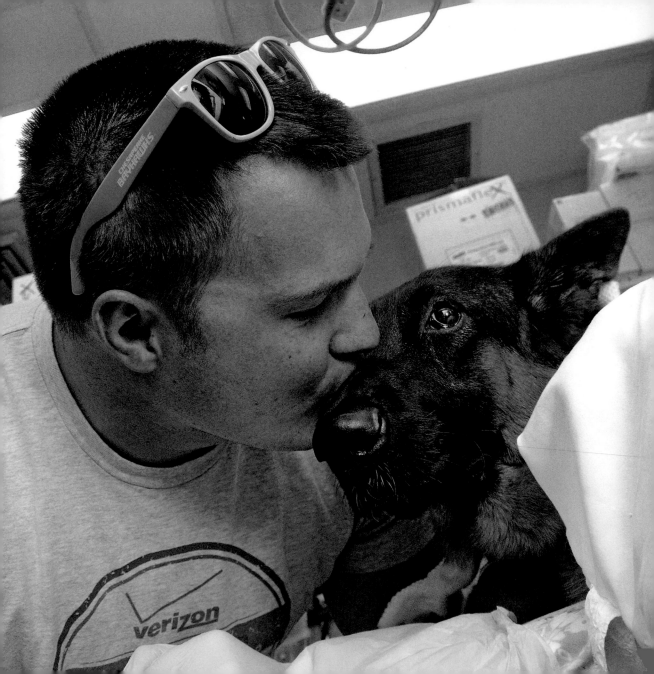

Gabriel

German shepherd ▪ Texas

★ ★ ★ ★ ★ ★ ★ ★ ★ ★ ★

There are great service dogs. And there are great service dog owners. A German shepherd named Gabriel and a West Point graduate and U.S. Army captain named Jake Murphy are examples of both.

Murphy was at the end of an 18-month stay at Walter Reed Medical Center, recovering from a double leg amputation caused by an improvised explosive device (IED) in Afghanistan, when he applied for a service dog. "I'd always had a dog growing up," Murphy says. "And while I wasn't suffering from PTSD, I didn't know if I would need physical help down the road."

While Murphy awaited a match, his wife, Lisa, received a call from someone asking if she knew a veteran who was interested in a service dog. The dog's intended owner, U.S. Army Sgt. Derek McConnell, had recently passed away. The caller had no idea that Murphy and McConnell were not only friends, but they had also been deployed together and were injured on the same day. After McConnell escorted Murphy safely to the medevac, he went back out on patrol and stepped on an IED, which caused the loss of his legs.

The pair had spent more than a year at Walter Reed together before McConnell's death. Murphy was mourning the loss of his friend when

OPPOSITE: *Gabriel embraces the affection of his owner to whom his match seems fated.*

Lisa got word that 4 Paws for Ability, a training facility in Xenia, Ohio, was trying to place Gabriel. "When we were together in the hospital, Derek was emailing the trainer every day asking for pictures of Gabriel," Murphy remembers. "I felt like I knew him."

When Murphy was released from the hospital, he and Lisa brought Gabriel to Texas, where Murphy had gotten a job. "Sometimes in the morning when I have to put on my prosthetics, I think it sucks that I lost my legs, but there's nothing I can do about it," he says of his attitude. "You can wallow in pity, but life isn't like a movie where you can skip past the parts you don't like." Murphy initially brought Gabriel to work with him, but as Murphy mastered his prosthetics, the canine assistance proved unnecessary. He no longer needed Gabriel's help to pick up something he'd dropped, and he didn't suffer from PTSD for which the dog might lend emotional comfort. Plus, Gabriel had trouble sitting still. So Murphy transitioned Gabriel into the role of family dog.

Gabriel soon adjusted to staying home with Lisa and chasing tennis balls and long walks. "He turned out to be a wonderful pet with amazing manners," says Murphy. But only a few months into his enjoyable new routine, Gabriel fell into a pond and was soon acting lethargic. He was diagnosed with leptospirosis, a rare but deadly disease he had caught from bacteria in the water.

> "You can wallow in pity, but life isn't like a movie where you can skip past the parts you don't like."

AMERICAN ICON International movie star Rin Tin Tin, a German shepherd rescued from a World War I battlefield, helped popularize the handsome and highly intelligent breed in the United States. At the peak of his silent film career in the 1920s, the four-legged celebrity—whose fame contributed to the success of Warner Brothers—received as many as 10,000 fan letters weekly.

Gabriel surprised the veterinarians by surviving, but he endured weeks of costly dialysis. Now, Murphy comes home from work, greets his wife and young son, and spends half an hour administering a bag of IV fluid to the dog. "We're incredibly bonded," Murphy says. And while he admits Gabriel doesn't have the "it" factor for service, "What Gabriel *does* have is the good dog factor. I love him so much." ★

Still healing from illness, Gabriel rests on the lawn with a prized tennis ball.

Alli

ON THE TRAIL TO PROTECTING ANIMALS

Australian cattle dog mix ■ Washington

★ ★ ★ ★ ★ ★ ★ ★ ★ ★ ★ ★

Most dogs have an uncanny ability to locate a long-buried bone, a piece of cheese left at the bottom of a bag, something pungent in which to roll. But Alli ups the ante: She can find a frog a foot underwater, detect a Pacific pocket mouse's diminutive scat, and identify the even tinier scat of an endangered caterpillar. Not bad for a cattle dog mix who flunked out of a drug detection program because of what seemed like less-than-promising behavior.

Now Alli is a member of Conservation Canines, a program at the University of Washington's Center for Conservation Biology that rescues dogs and turns them into master wildlife CSI detectives. Once trained, the dogs are charged with locating endangered species so that they might be identified and studied. Program coordinator Heath Smith oversees the training of the pups, who travel the globe in search of tigers in Cambodia, bears in the French Pyrenees, orcas in the San Juan Islands, and jaguars in Mexico.

Smith selects the dogs with two imperatives: They must be rescues and they must be willing to play ball—literally and obsessively. "Want to fetch?" is Smith's only measure of a potential

OPPOSITE: *Clad in her Ruffwear vest, supersniffer Alli is ready to get to work for Conservation Canines.*

CATTLE DOG

) **Origin:** As the name suggests, this breed was developed to herd cattle. It blends a dingo's compact build and athleticism with a dalmatian's faithful protectiveness.

) **Temperament:** These high-energy dogs love having a job to do. They are easygoing but are also courageous and intelligent. Though wary of strangers, they develop close bonds with family.

) **Appearance:** Cattle dog coats are thick, smooth, and bluish gray or reddish gray in appearance.

canine's initial skill set. When he visits a shelter, a dog has to show Smith an insatiable drive to retrieve, a game that will become the reward for his or her work.

While she proved an adept fetcher, Alli, who had been trained to detect drugs, didn't have a résumé that suggested star potential. She was skittish around people, and she had a tendency to nip those with whom she did interact. But Smith adopted Alli anyway, knowing that Conservation Canines' remote work locations would keep her socially isolated, and that otherwise she might be euthanized due to her aggressive tendencies.

Within one day of training, Alli was showing exceptional skill at identification. She quickly learned to recognize 300 individual samples in an exercise that asked the dogs to distinguish individual bears by their scat, ignoring the 20 or so samples that weren't correct and signaling to the one that was. Though identifications can be verified with genetics, DNA testing was much more expensive at the time Smith began work with Alli than rescuing a dog and taking a day to teach it what to do. The training is simple: Give the dog a sample of scat to smell. Then, continue to move it farther away until it is hidden or mixed in with other samples. When the dog identifies it correctly, throw a ball as a reward. Repeat.

The dogs, says Smith, instinctively want to work. "A lot of people think about how to command a dog to do what *you* want, but it's about how you can command a dog to do what it naturally does, and then manipulate that drive so it naturally does what you want it to." Smith teaches basic obedience commands along the way, but from day one, the dog is off

Alli and Smith scour the wilderness for evidence of the rare animals they seek to protect.

Alli sticks close to her handler and number one pal in northwest Washington.

Smith refers to as his "pumpkin" because of her coloring, even lived with her trainer for two years while she recovered from a torn ligament in her knee, rather than in the program's kennels. Now she relishes the company of both her human and canine colleagues.

"She's learned to trust people and she's supersweet," says Smith, who hands newcomers a tennis ball to throw to Alli to help make her comfortable. And she's abandoned her nipping habit for a more welcome show of affection: nibbling on ears and kissing. Smith adds with a smile, "She's gone from taking little bites out of people to killing you with kisses."

Professionally, Alli is all business, and Smith praises her gentle and careful manner. She has tracked wolves, wolverines, and grizzly bears, and she is also an expert at finding what is undetectable to the human eye. In the quest for an endangered caterpillar in Oregon, Smith had only a few days to teach Alli to find the scat, which he compares to a grain of pepper sprinkled on the floor. Every time Alli would find a sample during training, he remembers, her breath would blow it away. (Smith finally taped the samples down.) The first day on the job, they spent about an hour driving to

leash outdoors. "These are dogs who will never go far from the person holding the ball that they get to chase as a reward," he laughs.

As Alli learned her new job, she and Smith formed a devoted partnership. Alli, whom different locations where the caterpillar might be. "Just as I was thinking, 'Maybe not,'" Smith remembers, "she sat down and alerted. She ended up finding a ton of them."

Smith views the work of the program as a win-win: Not only is it saving dogs, but it also trains them to do essential work on a budget. When he was sent to Portugal to showcase the dogs' abilities, Smith simply went to a local shelter there and picked out a dog. After two weeks of training, the dog aced his presentation. As Smith says, "Our goal is to save as many dogs as possible and to have them be successful at their work."

Alli has now spent more than a decade on the job, during which time she has lived in the field with Smith or another handler from the program. Back in Washington State, the dogs are housed in the program's kennels, located across from the scientists' bunkhouse. For recreation, when the dogs aren't romping with each other, they join the scientists on bike rides and trips to swimming holes. "They have an amazing life," says Smith, "which is probably why so many of them are working when they are still 13 and 14 years old."

When the dogs do reach retirement age, they move in with their handlers. Two dogs who suffer from arthritis, Tucker and Sadie, continue to work on the orca project in Washington's San Juan Islands because they can do so from a boat, while others visit schools as part of education programs. It's a sweet final chapter for formerly imperiled dogs who are saved by their ability to safeguard other endangered species.

As for Smith, he calls his work saving wildlife with Alli and another Australian cattle dog rescue, Gator, the pinnacle of his career. For all involved, it is the ultimate reward for games of fetch well played. ★

THE NOSE KNOWS The moist spongy texture on dogs' superpowered noses catches scents from the air, and the nostrils work independently to allow dogs to determine the direction from which a scent came. Canines create distinct odor profiles to familiarize a place, even using scent residues to detect past presences or to predict future visitors whose scents are carried by wind.

Jericho

PULLING MORE THAN HIS WEIGHT

Pit bull ■ Maryland

★ ★ ★ ★ ★ ★ ★ ★ ★ ★ ★ ★

Jericho can pull a wheelchair, retrieve objects, and relieve himself on command. The only thing this rescue pit bull turned model service dog can't do for his person, Matthew Smith, is pretend to be brave.

When Smith's Maryland home was invaded in the middle of the night, Jericho alerted Smith to the fact that something was wrong. Since Jericho was naturally a quiet dog, Smith had had to train him to bark. So when Jericho barked that night, Smith knew something was wrong. Smith went to the door, and a man started pushing his way into the house. "We were fighting—I was beating him with my crutch, and it was getting louder," Smith describes. "Jericho ran behind my wife and peed on the floor."

Jericho's temperament makes him a terrible guard dog but a perfect service animal for Smith, who has relied on a wheelchair for more than two decades following a motorcycle crash. He began looking for canine assistance in 2013, after years of using a wheelchair and crutches resulted in torn rotator cuffs, arthritis, and bursitis.

A friend connected him with Animal Farm Foundation, a nonprofit organization in Dutchess County, New York, that trains rescue pit bulls to be service dogs. The organization's

OPPOSITE: *A patient and intuitive pit bull, Jericho sets the standard for assisting people with disabilities.*

certified Assistance Dogs International trainer, Apryl Lea, visited Smith's home with a dog whose skills she wanted to show as an example. Both Lea and Smith understood that training any dog for Smith would be complicated by the need for it to pull Smith in a wheelchair but *not* pull him on crutches.

Several months later, Lea called Smith to let him know she was training a dog she hoped would be a perfect match. Rescued from a high-kill shelter in Florida, Jericho had the strength to pull Smith's wheelchair and support his six-foot-four-inch frame. He also had a disposition the likes of which Lea had never seen: innate service-dog behavior even in public. Because pit bulls are such social animals, they often have difficulty ignoring someone who tries to make contact, says Lea, but Jericho naturally knew when he was working. "He's a big cuddler," she admits. "But nothing fazes him, and he has an instinct to have a job."

While Lea accepts her temporary role in the lives of the dogs that she trains, she admits that Jericho is one she would have kept.

After 10 months of training, Jericho was ready to live with Smith, who says from their first meeting it was as if they had always been together. "He was loving, he listened to me, he looked directly into my eyes, and he listened to my commands." Those commands include one to press buttons, another to relieve himself outside, and a request to retrieve. If Smith drops his keys, Jericho, thinking it's a game, grabs them. Smith drops them occasionally just for Jericho's entertainment. One skill Jericho is still working on is hitting the handicap button to open doors. "He hits them but he jumps up and slaps them as if he was giving someone a high ten," Smith says. "So I'm trying to teach him to touch it with his nose. He gets so grumpy when he's tried so many times he's like a teenager. He'll bite the button out of frustration."

DOGS AS MEDICINE Pet companionship can have significant health benefits: The blood pressure reduction achieved by living with a dog is thought to equal the reduction achieved by limiting salt or alcohol intake. Elderly dog owners also make fewer doctor visits per year than nonowners.

In addition to improving Smith's mobility, Jericho can make him comfortable in any environment.

Jericho, whom Smith describes as a "big goofy but beautiful dork," has accompanied Smith and his wife as far as Alaska. Yet it's his constant daily companionship that has altered Smith's life. While he had never considered the emotional benefits of a service dog, Smith says Jericho has eased his social anxiety. "Whenever you're disabled you always feels like eyes are on you, and when you're alone you don't have anyone to take attention off that feeling." But with Jericho, Smith explains, it's like having another person always with him who understands how he's feeling. Smith appreciates how Jericho puts his front paws in Smith's lap to be pet when he senses that he needs him, and also how Jericho helps him interact with strangers.

At home, Jericho is part of a loving triangle, watching TV on the couch with Smith and his wife. "He always wants to be the center of attention," says Smith, and that's fine with him. "He's just perfect. It's like the gates of heaven opened up and I was given this dog." ★

Beethoven

A SENSE FOR UNDERSTANDING

American bulldog shar-pei mix ▪ Georgia

★ ★ ★ ★ ★ ★ ★ ★ ★ ★ ★

Warden Dane Collins was looking for creative ways to overhaul the Muscogee County Jail's program for mental health inmates. Prisoners in the Columbus, Georgia, facility were receiving 10 weekly hours of counseling from a therapist, but it wasn't sufficient, according to Collins. "Jail's a tough place to be, especially if you have a mental illness," he says. "And the inmates get tired of listening to the same person talk all the time."

The psychologist who ran the program had a therapy dog that would go to hospitals and nursing homes, and something clicked for Collins. "Heck, why don't we try that in jail?" he remembers thinking. It wouldn't require law enforcement training, and the conditions of the right candidate were simple: a friendly dog who doesn't bite.

The jail already had a service dog named Marley, a golden Labrador in charge of sniffing out contraband, but Collins—who has two rescue dogs at home—was determined to rescue another. He enlisted Lt. Shanon Zeisloft to be the handler, and she and Marley's handler, Sgt. Gary DePetro, eagerly began visiting shelters. When Zeisloft saw Beethoven, she knew

OPPOSITE: *Beethoven, a deaf, mixed-breed dog rescued from a shelter, quickly mastered the skills of a therapy dog.*

she had found the perfect match in the mutt (a subsequent DNA test proved him to be a mix of American bulldog, shar-pei, Alaskan malamute, bullmastiff, and terrier).

The staff at PAWS Humane cautioned that Beethoven was deaf, but Zeisloft understood that this quality was only a bonus. "That makes him less susceptible to all the noise in the jail. Plus he's such a beautiful dog," she adds. "The dog has to have a good appearance and be friendly, because a lot of people are afraid of dogs." Zeisloft and DePetro took Beethoven for a walk around the shelter's grounds. The next day Zeisloft filled out the paperwork to adopt him.

Next came the work of figuring out how to train a deaf dog to pass the American Kennel Club Canine Good Citizen test for certification. Collins admits he was nervous, but Zeisloft reassured him Beethoven could do it. When she found a local trainer who turned out also to have a deaf dog, Zeisloft was elated.

By the end of six months of training, Beethoven had learned numerous sign commands, including the trick of playing dead, and he passed his therapy dog test on the first try. Now he visits four dorms a week to spend time with mental health inmates and veterans. It's a job Zeisloft says Beethoven loves as much as his off-duty time. He also volunteers at Columbus Hospice, Orchard Nursing Home, and a few local public schools and libraries where children, unaware that he is deaf, practice reading to him.

But it's Beethoven's time in jail that Zeisloft says makes him race to work. "When he gets his vest on and we start going down the hallway to see the inmates, he'll begin to run there." As for the inmates, "They play with him and hug him. It's the highlight of their week. I think it really does help them escape their reality in jail"—a jail that has ultimately given a formerly doomed dog his freedom. ★

THE TELLTALE TAIL Studies have shown that the direction a tail wags is an emotional cue. Asymmetry is believed to be a reflection of hemispheric activity in the brain: Left-brain activation produces a wag to the right, signaling a positive response to friendly or familiar stimuli. Right-brain activation produces a leftward wag, indicating a negative response to a perceived threat or something unknown.

Beethoven gets a double thumbs-up from an inmate. He is trained to follow visual commands.

Lyric

Mango lovers, beware: If you are trying to sneak one back to the mainland from the San Juan airport, you're likely to be busted by a dog named Lyric. The hardworking beagle is on one of more than 120 active dog-and-handler teams in the United States Department of Agriculture's Beagle Brigade.

AIRPORT SECURITY MADE SWEET

Beagle ■ San Juan, Puerto Rico

Despite her sweet face and constantly wagging tail, Lyric is (mostly) all business when she's at work. After being recruited as a rescue into the USDA's program, Lyric went through extensive physical and temperament testing before beginning her 10-week training.

Lyric is heralded for her rapid learning, which she proved within days by identifying in record time luggage that contained prohibited produce. "Her willingness to work is so high and she is so fast at finding things," says her handler, Jorge Torres. Unlike dogs who work at a luggage carousel, Lyric does her job at airport gates. Surprisingly, with the endless distractions of people eating and children running around, Lyric isn't thrown off the scent by smelly deli sandwiches or a game of tag. "Her only problem is too much attention," Torres laughs. "If someone says, 'What a cute dog!' she can get distracted by the hope of a good rub or scratch."

Michael Smith, the director of the USDA's National Detector Dog Training Center in Georgia, says beagles' friendliness, keen sense of smell, and high food drive make them ideal sniffers in social environments such as airports. "The only downside is they're stubborn, so sometimes they could smell something that's not a target odor like dirty socks," says Smith. "And they'll refuse to go anywhere."

Lyric's natural gifts and charm make her a star in the airport as well as Torres's favorite colleague. "She loves me, and I love her." ★

OPPOSITE: *An adorable contraband detector, Lyric sits beside luggage she has inspected at the airport.*

Bell

BRINGING PEACE TO A WAR VETERAN

Labradoodle ■ Texas

★ ★ ★ ★ ★ ★ ★ ★ ★ ★ ★ ★

A dog can be the best medicine. In the case of a Labradoodle named Bell, she's better than any medicine. Army Lt. Col. Brian Weber, a physician assistant who spent more than 30 years in the army, is one of many to benefit from that special healing power.

One month before Weber's deployment to Afghanistan in 2005, his 18-year-old son was in a car accident; after 16 days in the ICU, he was removed from life support and buried. In Afghanistan, a mourning Weber struggled with the combat around him. "I was working, working, working all the time," he remembers. When he returned home to Commerce, Texas, one year later, Weber and his wife divorced.

"I wasn't sleeping, I was irritable, I wouldn't talk to anybody," says Weber, who was working in a family practice at the time. Diagnosed with PTSD, Weber started counseling and medication regimens, but they had little effect. When a fellow veteran told him about the comfort he had found in a dog from Patriot PAWS, an organization that trains service dogs for veterans, Weber decided to fill out an application. "I was tired of being alone," Weber recalls. Although he had trained

OPPOSITE: *Bell's warm presence calms Weber through tense moments and restless nights.*

chocolate Labradors for duck hunting in the past, Weber knew he no longer had the patience for a puppy and would need a trained service dog. He also understood that the wait time would be a one- to two-year minimum, but after filling out the paperwork, he requested an informational interview as soon as possible. "I wanted them to know I was serious," he explains. "The moment I walked in their door, it was like I was home. We did the official interview right there."

He prepared himself for the inevitable wait, but Patriot PAWS called the next day: A dog named Bell had just been returned to them because her owner was in the hospital with terminal cancer and could no longer care for her. The next week, Weber was in the office face-to-face with the bearded blonde Labradoodle—a mix of the friendly Labrador retriever and the highly intelligent poodle. When Weber fed Bell out of his hand, she put her head on his lap and looked at him. "That was that," Weber says. "I fell in love."

> When Weber fed Bell out of his hand, she put her head on his lap and looked at him. "That was that," Weber says. "I fell in love."

Weber began daily drives—40 minutes each way—during his lunch break to train with Bell. Three months later, Patriot PAWS asked if he wanted to try taking Bell home. At the time, he was still having nightmares, but that first night, "She put her head on my lap and she took it away," Weber remembers. "She's taken all my nightmares away."

By day, Bell is the star of the family practice office. Not much of a morning dog, Bell doesn't like getting up early to go to work—she puts a paw over her eyes when Weber wakes her—but she thrives on the attention once she's in the office. "I have patients who make appointments just to see Bell," Weber says of his sweet-tempered companion. "She gets very connected to the babies and older folks. And people tend to open up a bit more around her, which is incredible." In 2015, the Texas Veterinary Medical Foundation voted Bell "professional dog of the year" in honor of her remarkable impact in a place of healing.

If Weber begins to grow tense or, as he describes, "drift back to Afghanistan," Bell will plant herself in front of him and demand eye contact or nudge him. "She has a deep, loving, soulful look that lets you know everything is OK," he explains. "And she doesn't hesitate to put that big wet cold nose on me somewhere and say, 'Hey!'"

Weber now has a girlfriend, but he also enjoys date nights with his favorite furry girl. He and Bell attend the symphony together and sit by the string section where there's more room, and they frequently go out for dinner together. On the weekends, they go running and fish side by side. And when they are back home, Weber no longer feels dread about going to bed with Bell beside him. "The only way I know I've had a bad night is that Bell is pretty tired the next day," he says.

The relief that Bell has brought Weber goes beyond his ability to sleep. Only 10 months into life with his companion, Weber went off all of his medications and has not looked back. "I'm not anxious anymore. I don't need sleeping pills, I don't need anything," he says in amazement. "I only got Bell for companionship, but she is a miracle." ★

Bell offers Weber a paw at the family practice office where she has become a friend to staff and patients.

Duke

A CANINE COWBOY

Border collie ■ Nebraska

★ ★ ★ ★ ★ ★ ★ ★ ★ ★ ★ ★

Sometimes, it all comes down to a look in the eye. That's what saved Duke, a rescued border collie who changed the life of a Nebraska cattle farmer named Troy Balderston, who was looking for a little extra help in the field.

When a family found the border collie wandering in Saint Joseph, Missouri, they called Jackie Allenbrand, a cattle farmer and founder of Pets Helping Agriculture in Rural Missouri (PHARM Dog USA), a nonprofit based in Stanberry, Missouri, that trains and places service dogs with disabled farmers. Since 2009, PHARM has provided more than 15 trained dogs to disabled farmers across the Midwest. When Allenbrand received the call, she was in the process of looking for a canine helper for Balderston. She also happened to be down the road, doing a demonstration at a tractor supply store with Bobby Miller, who trains and donates border collies to the organization. Allenbrand and Miller told the family that if they could come by with Duke, they would assess him.

They knew instantly that they had a winner. Successful working border collies have something called the "eye," which Miller describes as a stare and focus that on its own can move an animal: "You take a 35- to 40-pound dog

OPPOSITE: *Duke's energy and eagerness to work let Balderston continue his career in cattle farming.*

A personalized car tag boasts the talents of working border collies.

"away to me" to drive the animals in the required direction. Not all border collies share the herding drive: "If they're not born with that instinct, I can't put it there. But Duke had it," Miller explains.

Given the will to work, Miller says the training process isn't rocket science; the dogs know what to do and simply need the right conditions and situations in which to perform. "My daughter is really, really smart," he laughs. "But I have a bumper sticker that says, 'My border collie is smarter than your honor roll student.'" In addition to patience and consideration, Miller notes that the most important training ingredient is love. "You have to love them or it doesn't work."

Duke went to Iowa to finish his training with Don McKay, who worked him with cattle to suit the needs of his intended owner, Troy Balderston. Left quadriplegic by an automobile accident in 2010, the father of two young children was unable to continue working on his own at his feed yard where he raised calves. In 2012, a friend offered him a job at his feed-lot, cattle operation, and crop-growing farm just across the border in Kansas. Adjustments were made to the farm to make it more

and you put him against a thousand-pound cow—he's got to convince them he's meaner than they are." Remembers Allenbrand, "Duke got into the store, looked at the sheep, and started crawling towards him. We said. 'Yes, we want him!'"

Miller took Duke home and spent several weeks working him with his sheep, teaching him such commands as "down," "come by," and accessible for Balderston—such as easier-to-open gates and squeeze chutes—but he still found himself at a disadvantage. The cattle displayed little respect for him seated in a wheelchair below them, and his all-terrain wheelchair didn't move at the speed necessary to control the animals.

Then, the AgrAbility program at the University of Nebraska–Lincoln, which is dedicated to serving the state's farm and ranch families affected by disabilities, suggested he consider a PHARM USA dog. "I agreed because I'd take any sort of tool I could use to get back to doing what I used to do," says Balderston.

Before Duke's fortuitous rescue from the streets, Balderston might have been looking at a wait of as long as two years. Miller, who donates both the dogs and his training services, works with the dogs as puppies but doesn't begin "real" training until they are about one and a half years old. But because Duke was already at least a year old, Miller told Balderston he could probably have him ready in six months, adding the caveat: "You have to match the dog to the farmer. The dog has to work and be happy."

Six months of phone calls and exchanged pictures later, Balderston met Duke. Allenbrand, her husband, and McCay drove him to the farm in July 2013. "The first thing he did when he got out of the pickup was come straight to me," Balderston remembers. "He just come up and sat down and put his nose on my hand, and I pet him." Allenbrand remembers being surprised that Duke ran to Balderston after the long drive rather than to McCay,

FOUR-LEGGED SHEPHERDS With their trademark "herding eye," border collies were bred as sheepdogs in the border area of England and Scotland (hence their name). The breed's working style comes from a standout herder named Old Hemp, whose quiet yet tireless efficiency made him a reigning champion at Britain's sheepdog trials. Generations of border collies have been bred from Old Hemp's genes, with an emphasis on working ability over looks. The herding instinct in these remarkably smart, energetic dogs is so strong that they will try to direct anything from blowing leaves to other animals, such as cats, rabbits, and ducks.

BORDER COLLIE

- **Origin:** Sheepherding is one of the oldest jobs in the dog world. Breeders taught dogs to forgo their predator instincts and protect livestock that would have otherwise been their prey.
- **Training Tip:** Border collies can learn a huge vocabulary of hundreds of words and are trained with clear, repeated commands.
- **Appearance:** These muscular medium-size dogs are built for agility and endurance.

who had been training him. "It was like he knew that Troy was his farmer," she says. "And he was there to help."

Soon Duke and Balderston, working as a team, were able to gather cattle on the pasture faster than the mounted cowboys. Duke can bring individual animals right to Balderston, whereas Balderston once had to chase them in his wheelchair. "If there's a sick calf, Duke and I can go into the feedlot and get the sick one out," he says. "He's allowed me to get back to what I love doing, which is working with cattle."

In addition to his herding help, Duke is trained to assist with specific needs relating to Balderston's disability. Because Balderston can't maneuver quickly, Duke's duties include ensuring Balderston's safety among the cattle. In tight spaces, Duke keeps the cattle from getting too close to Balderston. Of this counterintuitive skill, Miller explains, "Training the dogs to drive the cattle or sheep away from the person goes against their natural instinct to bring things to you, so that's the last command they learn."

Allenbrand and Miller say Duke is like the other border collies they have owned, loved, and placed—not only in his drive and desire to work, but also in his attachment to his human partner. "Their reward at the end of the day," says Miller of the breed, "is being with you." And while Duke prefers to retreat to his doghouse come bedtime rather than joining the family in their home, he is waiting by the pickup truck first thing in the morning, ready to go to work. "He goes *everywhere* with me," says Balderston of his companion. "We have other guys at the farm and they want his help, but he won't leave my side." ★

Duke rests after an active day chasing cattle. After work he assists Balderston at home, too.

Zeke took a bullet for his team at the Harrisburg, Pennsylvania, police department. And even then, as the Belgian Malinois went into shock from a gunshot wound to his neck, Zeke refused to leave the suspect.

For 15 months leading to this moment, Zeke had assisted his handler, Cpl. Tyron Meik, in the recovery of drugs, firearms, and money, as well as in making arrests. On this particular day, the pair was tasked with tracking a suspect in a stabbing and shooting. "I put his harness on and Zeke was like, 'Dad, let's do this,'" Meik recalls. He looked to the sky and prayed his dog wouldn't get shot, and they got on the trail.

When Zeke had tracked the suspect to within 10 yards, Meik called to the perpetrator, "Let me see your hands!" The suspect was running up a fallen tree, so Zeke jumped and grabbed his right knee. A gunshot sounded next. Meik ran closer and saw that Zeke's blood was everywhere. Despite his grave injury, Zeke held on to the man who had shot him until Meik removed him.

Meik stayed with his dog until help arrived in the form of an emergency helicopter. "I just kept saying, 'Hold on, buddy, don't die on me,'" Meik remembers. "I was losing my mind."

Thanks to exemplary vet care and his own tenacity, Zeke was back at work six weeks later and ready to play at home. Today he counts dozens of arrests and the recovery of thousands of dollars among his career achievements.

"He loves every minute of life," Meik says. The star police dog is particularly fond of tug-of-war, which Meik plays both to reward him and to wear him out. Zeke's other favorite treat is a sock—dirty or clean—that he'll sleep with in his mouth. Even the bravest beings need their occasional comforts. ★

Zeke

FEARLESS HELPER TO THE POLICE FORCE

Belgian Malinois ■ Pennsylvania

OPPOSITE: *Tireless police dog Zeke has faced many dangers, including gunfire, while aiding the force.*

Eudy & Tula

PROTECTORS OF PENGUINS

Maremma sheepdogs ■ Victoria, Australia

★ ★ ★ ★ ★ ★ ★ ★ ★ ★ ★ ★

A 3.7-acre island in Australia is still home to little penguins, the smallest of the penguin species, thanks to the supervision of two Maremma sheepdogs named Eudy and Tula whose life mission is protecting the birds.

Between 2000 and 2005, about a hundred birds a year were being lost to foxes that ventured to the island whenever low tides made it accessible from the Warrnambool mainland on Victoria's southwestern coast. Then, a staggering 360 birds were lost in two nights, leaving the total population at only six birds—down from 800 in 1999. The Warrnambool city council needed to do something fast or risk losing the species altogether.

A local chicken farmer named Allan Marsh suggested that they borrow his Maremma sheepdog, Oddball. A breed used to protect chickens from foxes, Maremmas are known for bonding with the species they protect, unlike herding dogs. "People laughed at the idea at first," says Peter Abbott, the town's head of tourism. "But since the day that dog came to the island, we haven't lost a single bird."

Oddball became a local hero and even the star of an eponymous documentary film before retiring to his farm. That's when a pair

OPPOSITE: *Faithful sheepdogs and local icons Eudy and Tula guard endangered penguins on a wild island.*

MAREMMA SHEEPDOG

- **Origin:** Maremmas were bred in the pastures of Italy to be guardians, not pets. The dogs instinctively bond with livestock—usually sheep, goats, alpacas, or llamas—and have a secondary bond with their human owners.
- **Temperament:** These sheepdogs are attentive, independent, and trustworthy. Though good natured, they may become territorial and defensive if kept in a house.
- **Training Tip:** Exposing newly weaned puppies to livestock helps bond them with their adopted families.

of female siblings named Tula and Eudy took up the guard, with Abbott and Phil Root, the city council–appointed dog handler, serving as their caretakers.

When Tula and Eudy first met the penguins, they were puppies, which eased them into island life and becoming accustomed to the smell of the penguins so it became "normal." As adults with an instinct to guard, they protect the penguins around the clock five days a week; the other two days they spend on the mainland watching over the chickens at the maritime village.

Abbott remembers the dogs reacting to a hawk circling over a lone chick that had left its nest. One barked at Abbott until he followed her toward her partner watchdog, who was stationed beside the endangered chick. The dogs also sound the alert by barking if boats or people are too close to the island.

Maremma aren't ideal pets, according to Abbott, because of their dominant and sometimes aloof personalities—not to mention the barking. "But there is a bond between Phil and myself and the dogs," Abbott says. "They understand we're looking after them."

When he and Root arrive on their daily visits to check in and feed Tula and Eudy, they're met with pure joy: The dogs stand and wag their tails, flop on their backs for belly rubs, and play games. "The care of the dogs is really a love job, and Phil and I have crossed well over the line of seeing them as working dogs," Abbott says. "I have a golden retriever at home who tries to be brave like a Maremma, but really he is a big sook"—Aussie slang for whiner—"and I think he knows I am seeing other dogs behind his

Eudy and Tula and their caretaker peer over Middle Island's banks from a scenic perch.

back. And my kids say I talk about Eudy and Tula more than I talk about them."

Abbott and Root's attachment to the dogs means worrying about Tula during the thunderstorms that scare her, and returning to the island when both dogs occasionally wander off during low tide and stroll about the town. The police always call when they see them, but not before snapping a selfie with the local stars, Abbott adds.

Tula and Eudy's fame extends far beyond Warrnambool, in part thanks to the film about Oddball. As a result, "Tula" and "Eudy" have become stage names of sorts, with Abbott and Root referring to them by different monikers so that the dogs don't respond to calling fans.

Now that the penguin population has rebounded to 180, the community is convinced of the Maremma defense system. Not that it has been a hard-won battle, Abbott admits, adding, "We're saving very cute penguins with very cute dogs." ★

Zoey

SCHOOLED IN THE ART OF COMFORT

Golden retriever ■ Wisconsin

★ ★ ★ ★ ★ ★ ★ ★ ★ ★ ★ ★

College students far from home often miss their pets even more than their parents, which makes Zoey's presence on the Concordia University Wisconsin's Mequon campus all the more profound. The golden retriever is a university-employed comfort dog, who is trained to be of service to the community.

A presentation from the Lutheran Church Charities (LCC) sparked the idea of a campus dog for Dave Enters, the school's director of counseling services. LCC had developed a program that pairs dogs with ministry missions after observing the extraordinary connection many people share with their pets. When the group responded to the Hurricane Katrina disaster, LCC's president Tim Hetzner watched local residents refuse FEMA's rescue efforts because the organization wouldn't take dogs and they couldn't leave their companions. At the site of other traumatic events, Hetzner also noticed that long lines of people would form to see comfort dogs. So the ministry began inviting volunteers with certified therapy dogs to join them when members responded to disaster areas, and in 2008, the organization began training its own dogs.

Today, LCC has trained more than a hundred K-9 Comfort Dogs, as they are called, and has

OPPOSITE: *Zoey's gift for empathy makes her a boon to college students going through tough times.*

Zoey welcomes attention with a K-9 Comfort Dog vest and a Green Bay Packers collar.

Zoey is the first dog to be placed at a university and given a full-time job description. She works side by side with 10 handlers and alternates between living with two of them. Thanks to Zoey's upbringing, she thrives on the frequent changing of the guard. While most dogs latch on to one human leader instinctively, Enters says Zoey has been trained to have multiple alphas. Since she understands that whoever is holding the leash is "top dog," the team has a transition process during which one handler passes the leash to the next so that Zoey can make the mental adjustment. "The necessary ingredient in the handler and comfort dog relationship is that Zoey trusts and respects every one of us," Enters adds. "She has 12 very best friends."

placed them in 22 states. The dogs are also on hand to travel to disaster sites and have volunteered in the aftermath of the shootings in Newtown, Connecticut, and the Boston Marathon bombing. Each dog even has its own Facebook page, explains Hetzner, "So that people can continue to talk to that dog on social media almost as if it were a counselor. The handlers have to do the responding, of course, but many people are just more comfortable talking to a dog."

Accompanied by those friends, Zoey—who responds to more than 50 commands—roams the hallways, allows students to pet her, goes into classrooms for presentations on stress relief, and is present in Enters's office when students come to speak with him. Off campus, she performs community outreach in nursing homes, hospitals, schools, and camps. Hetzner praises her work on and off campus. "Zoey is an example for the students of what it means to be a caring, loving, contributing member of society. Dogs are really good teachers."

Zoey's ability to listen has most impressed Enters, who frequently brings Zoey to work. After 35 years in the counseling field, Enters has witnessed the months it can take to build rapport with students, but with a dog in the room, he says, there can be an immediate bridge for conversation. "There are traumas that people experience in life, such as being sexually or physically assaulted, that are at times almost impossible to talk about," he explains. "But with Zoey, they can." One student agreed to testify in court against the man who raped her, as long as Zoey could be by her side. She was.

When Zoey is "de-vested," or not at work, her favorite way to blow off steam is to tear boxes to shreds. At work she is rewarded with games of fetch. "One of the things we discovered early on is that when she's vested, she has an intentionally meek posture to be approachable, but some of the students interpret that as her being depressed or oppressed," he explains. To show Zoey's playful side, he gets students to play tug-of-war with her or to chase her.

"There's no question that Zoey and her presence enhance the emotional being of our campus," says Enters. "All you need to do is walk down the hallway when we're with her and see the expressions on the faces of the people who approach. They're always smiles." ★

Zoey's presence in counseling sessions relaxes students and facilitates conversation.

Hudson

AN ADVOCATE FOR ANIMALS

Pit bull ■ New York

★ ★ ★ ★ ★ ★ ★ ★ ★ ★ ★ ★

Hudson has gone from victim to advocate, thanks to his work alongside owner Richard Nash. In 2012, the three-week-old pit bull and his two littermates were found nailed to railroad tracks in Albany, New York. The dogs were rescued and taken to the Mohawk Hudson Humane Society for treatment.

Hudson ultimately lost a paw and his sister Pearl recovered, but the third sibling, Carina, died shortly after being rescued. The animal cruelty case drew international attention to the "railroad puppies," as the trio became known, but it would be a story with a happy ending.

Within weeks of adopting Hudson, Nash and his wife, Rosemarie, who live in Schodack, New York, were determined to make the pit bull a public face of goodwill. "We wanted to get him out there and show that you can overcome whatever life throws at you," Nash explains, adding that Hudson—who sports a prosthetic foot that attaches to his leg with Velcro—is a heartening example for anyone who is suffering.

Once Hudson received his therapy dog certification, the couple started visiting schools. Soon they began working as a team at a hospice. Hudson is adaptive to whatever the patients

OPPOSITE: *Despite suffering from abuse as a puppy, Hudson shows contagious enthusiasm for life.*

need, says Nash. "He will lie down so people can pet him, or some people want to shake his paw, or he likes to give puppy kisses. It depends on the person."

"Seeing a dog brings up memories," Nash says of the hospice visits. He remembers one woman who shared, for the first time, that she used to have a dog. It took her 10 minutes to remember her pet's name, according to Nash, but the breakthrough led to other details of her past. Afterward, the nurses told Nash that they had never known about the woman's childhood and explained that she may not have remembered herself until she saw Hudson.

As an activist, Hudson is a force. He and Nash are frequent visitors to the New York State Capitol, where they advocate for stricter animal cruelty laws. They also do what they can, in front of senators and Facebook fans alike, to change the perception of the oft-maligned pit bull breed. "There's a big stereotype, and we want to show that it's not the animal, it's how you raise them," says Nash.

According to his owner, Hudson is delighted to be of service. "If he didn't like it, I wouldn't do it, because it would be setting him up to fail." Instead, Hudson, who especially loves kissing children, is the one pulling Nash into the schools and other facilities where they volunteer. Although he struggles with stairs and getting in and out of Nash's truck, he has no problem jumping on the couch at home and settling in. A good thing, says Nash, given that, with political stumping and good works aside, "Hudson is the laziest dog who has ever lived." ★

EXTRAORDINARY SIDEKICK Author and activist Helen Keller, the first deaf-blind person to earn a bachelor of arts degree, had a well-known bull terrier. In her second year at Radcliffe College in Cambridge, Massachusetts, Keller visited a dog kennel with friends and met Sir Thomas. The skittish dog took to Keller instantly, placing his head in her lap and refusing to leave her side. Keller's peers secretly fund-raised to adopt the dog and present him as a gift. Sir Thomas became a faithful companion who escorted Keller around campus and patiently waited outside her classroom. Like Keller, he was loved throughout the community.

Hudson and Nash share the dog's inspiring story of resilience with New York schoolchildren.

For four years, Patches accompanied her owner, Brad Curtis, to his job as a crossing guard in Jersey Shore, Pennsylvania. Outfitted in a custom-made uniform that included a vest and a stop sign, the Maltipoo guaranteed the slowing of traffic as people paused for a better look.

For children on their way to and from school, Patches was always good for a pet and a kiss. "He's a much loved member of the town," says Curtis. "Having Patches here made people happy."

Curtis first brought Patches to work and left him in the car, but knowing that the dog's watchful eye meant he wanted out, Curtis finally let him stay by his side. Even without training to do so, the devoted pup watched Curtis's heels and followed his every move.

Stationed in front of the Country Beary Shack, Patches developed a taste for a certain reward for a job well done: bacon bits that the shop owner Lyra Clark fed him when he visited. Patches's telltale scratch at the door always signaled his arrival. "He's a little sweetheart," says Clark.

Patches

LOCAL CROSSWALK CELEBRITY

Maltipoo ▪ Pennsylvania

"And the kids look forward to seeing him every day. Some of the kids walking by don't have good lives, but he puts a smile on their faces."

In the fall of 2015, a local news channel story alerted the Jersey Shore Area School District to Patches's presence. School officials swiftly "fired" the beloved Maltipoo, citing school policy that it was illegal to have a dog in the crosswalk. Clark stepped up and hired Patches as a security guard and goodwill ambassador at the Country Beary Shack. "We found a way to make everybody happy," says Curtis.

Patches continues his community outreach as a certified therapy dog. He now goes into libraries, where children read anything but the letter of the law to him. That he's heard already. ★

OPPOSITE: *The petite Patches turns heads in her crosswalk uniform, making her a community fixture.*

Drago

OFFERING SOLACE AFTER TRAGEDY

Spinone Italiano ■ Connecticut

★ ★ ★ ★ ★ ★ ★ ★ ★ ★ ★ ★

On Friday, December 14, 2012, Adam Lanza opened fire at Sandy Hook Elementary School in Newtown, Connecticut, fatally shooting 20 children and six adult staff members. Four days later, the town's teachers and students were asked to return to their schools and resume classes.

"The time we stood waiting for the kids to get off the school bus that morning was surreal," says fifth-grade teacher Karen King of nearby Reed Intermediate School. "The teachers were crying because we didn't know what to do. We didn't know what to say to the children when they came in." The tragedy affected everyone in the small community, including a child in King's class who lost his sister.

While the teachers waited anxiously for their students, they started petting the therapy dogs that volunteers had brought to offer relief. The moment the students entered the building, King remembers, they exclaimed, "Oh my God! There are dogs in our school!" The students and teachers gathered around the canine comforters. "It was just about the dogs, and it was perfect," says King. "It was all the distraction we needed in that moment to feel safe." Those dogs, she says, are the untold story

OPPOSITE: *With his shaggy coat and gentle nature, Drago has an innate ability to lift spirits for kids and adults alike.*

A dapper Drago sports a tux in honor of the library's summer reading program kickoff.

wonderful when you're not wanting to kill him," she jokes. Friedman describes Drago as personable but slow to mature, both marks of the breed. "Sometimes he's adorable, but when he's competing in the ring for obedience and gets disqualified because it's time to stay and he decides to walk up to someone who looks like they need a hug, it's not necessarily so adorable." Yet whatever Drago's shortcomings in following directions, he more than makes up for it in social intuition, especially around children.

When Friedman, a nearby resident, heard the news of the shooting, she put her dogs in the car and drove to the crisis center to volunteer. She knew that having the dogs present would be helpful, explaining, "People gravitate to a creature who isn't going to judge them, and Drago will get close to them and touch them. It's unconditional love."

In the painful aftermath of the shootings, Drago sat at the ready to accompany people while they spoke with clergy or psychologists, or to entertain the children while their parents did. "People were just paralyzed and didn't know what to do, and Drago would sit there and lean against them," says Friedman.

of Newtown and how the community began finding ways to heal.

One dog in particular proved to be a hero at healing—if not necessarily heeling. Drago, a Spinone Italiano owned by Lauren Friedman, would roam those hallways and sit in the classrooms for the rest of the school year with Friedman's other Spinone, Siena.

Friedman certified Drago as a therapy dog when he turned one year old. "He's pretty

A few days later, Drago and Siena headed back to school to start spending time with the children in the classrooms. There, Drago's endearing habit of cocking his head quickly won over the students. King speculates that his goofy appearance and his heft, ideal for receiving enthusiastic hugs, helped. King began asking that Drago join her class daily as she read to the students. "Somehow he would know which kid needed him, and he would go plop down with him or her," she says. "When I talk to my kids about what they remember about that year, this is it. It was absolutely magical."

Drago—who would appear dressed in costume for holidays such as Valentine's Day and

> "People gravitate to a creature who isn't going to judge them, and Drago will get close to them and touch them."

Saint Patrick's Day—influenced the curriculum as well as his human peers. King remembers that a planned lesson on South America felt impossible both to teach and learn given the circumstances, so she instead assigned the children a research project on dog breeds. The student whose sister had been killed was tasked with interviewing the volunteering dogs and handlers. "He was really struggling," King remembers. "But he would go up to Drago and say, 'What's your favorite toy?' We didn't know how to make our way back to normal, so what the dogs did for us during that time was priceless."

Now that he is no longer needed at the school, Drago volunteers as an audience for children

EVOLVING FRIENDS Some 15,000 to 30,000 years ago, the domestication of wolves began. As the animals became our partners, the process altered their biology to give us the dogs we know today. Domestic dogs can read human expressions even though facial expressions aren't as important in communication with their own species. They learned our habit of pointing and, in a show of trust, will look to people for help with problem solving when needed.

SPINONE ITALIANO

) **Temperament:** Devoted, eager-to-please Spinones offer a steady stream of affection and communicate with softer grumbles or higher-pitched yodeling.

) **Training Tip:** The amiable pets need a lot of exercise but have a calmer temperament than most dogs bred for sporting.

) **Appearance:** Spinones' dense, wiry coats offer padding from harsh conditions, underbrush, and cold water to which they may be exposed while hunting.

learning to read in library programs and makes regular rounds at a Veterans Affairs (VA) hospital and a nursing home. Drago seems to be able to sense when people may soon pass away, Friedman says. "He'll motion to get on a bed in those cases—and if it is what the family wants, I'll allow him to—and he will just lie there with that person." For all his enthusiasm, he seems to sense when people are fragile.

Friedman admits that the jobs can be stressful on Drago. His reward for his work with humans is doing the work for which he was bred—tracking and hunting. (Drago's breed is the largest of the sporting dogs bred to hunt open game.) But most of the time when they're home, Friedman says, Drago and Siena nap. "It's not the breed for everyone," she admits. "They shed, and they drool—a lot. I have drool hanging from the walls. But they are patient, and tolerant, and kind. And all Drago wants to do is please."

As the Newtown community continues to heal, Drago's legacy endures. King has since rescued her own dog, as did the librarian and other colleagues. "We all thought they would be therapy dogs. It turns out they won't be that," she laughs. "But they're *our* therapy dogs." King is a strong supporter of Charlotte's Litter, a foundation begun in honor of Charlotte Helen Bacon, King's student's sister who was killed. Inspired by the dogs who tended to the living after the tragedy, the organization's goal is to provide therapy and comfort dogs to all who ask.

King believes that there is no environment that wouldn't benefit from a dog's presence, regardless of trauma. "We all muddle through things in an isolated way," she observes. But with dogs, "Words are not required. And everyone needs comfort." ★

Friedman poses with Drago and Siena in their Therapy Dogs International bandannas.

Judge

COMMITTED CRIME STOPPER

Czech shepherd ▪ New Jersey

★ ★ ★ ★ ★ ★ ★ ★ ★ ★ ★ ★ ★

It was not an auspicious beginning for a friendship, let alone a devoted partnership. Sgt. Michael Franks, an officer at the West Deptford Police Department in New Jersey, had always dreamed of being a K-9 handler, but he never imagined the likes of Judge, the 20-month-old Czech Shepherd with whom he was paired. Franks had championed a K-9 program in his department, writing a 30-page memo that was convincing enough to earn him a spot in patrol school. After requesting a "tough dog," he found himself beside Judge.

Days into the 18-week program, Judge was excelling. He had a strong work ethic, could perform tasks necessary for crowd control and building searches, and navigated wet floors and stairwells with ease. But when it came to apprehending people acting the parts of criminals in arrest scenarios, "He wouldn't let the person go," Franks remembers with a smile. "And when I would try to take him off the person, he would then turn and bite *me*." It happened five or six times, according to Franks, who made several trips to the emergency room and even received 10 stitches across his nose. But one of the ace trainers at the school told him, "If you

OPPOSITE: *Judge's achievements on the police force include apprehending suspects and recovering stolen items.*

can stick with it, I promise you will get a great dog." He and Judge worked things out. And he got a great dog.

During Judge's seven-year career on the force, he accompanied Franks on patrols and to the precinct, riding in the back of his van. Judge apprehended 152 suspects, helped recover three stolen vehicles, three firearms, and approximately $47,000 in reputed drug money. But Judge was equally valued for his less quantifiable job of buoying the officers' spirits, whether it was socializing in the precinct or making them feel protected. "I couldn't wait to go to work with him," Franks says. "Every day with him was exciting."

Off duty, Judge stayed just as close to Franks, even keeping guard while he slept. When Franks married and went on to have two children, Judge embraced family life. He was very protective, but when his collar was removed at the end of the workday, Franks says, Judge would "start racing around like it was Christmas. And in the morning, when it was time for work, he would put his game face back on."

Judge's weak spot was distance from Franks. When Franks would leave him in the van for even a brief amount of time, Judge's separation anxiety caused him to bite the bars of the kennel—hard. The resulting damage was four canine teeth that had to be replaced with titanium. When Judge snapped one of those teeth at the age of eight, Franks made the decision to retire him.

The first few days of watching Franks head to work without him, Judge clawed at and bit the door in a frenzy. He spent three weeks sitting in the bay window, refusing to move until his master got out of the car at the end of the day. "It was really tough in the beginning," Franks said. "But he was very close to my children and my wife, so eventually he just took to following them everywhere."

One year after his retirement, Judge was diagnosed with Cushing's disease. The endocrine disorder caused him to develop tumors and an intestinal blockage, and at one point he endured a surgery that resulted in 60 staples. Eventually, Judge was unable to eat or get up, and after three days of sleeping on the kitchen floor with him, Franks knew the time had come to euthanize him.

When Judge and Franks arrived at the animal hospital and prepared for their final walk together, Franks looked up and saw close to 100 saluting police officers lining the pathway. They had come from nearly every police department in the county, joining handlers and dogs from the Atlantic County K-9 academy who had come to say farewell to the team they had trained.

As Franks and Judge made their way through the officers who were standing in salute of their K-9 colleague, Judge joyfully picked up his favorite toy, a sleeve used for bite training. "Suddenly, it was as if nothing were wrong with him," Franks says. "It was like, 'I'll do this for you, Dad.'"

Franks, now a certified trainer for the K-9 academy, began working with his new charge—a Belgian Malinois named Tazor—during Judge's retirement. He says Tazor excels at police work but will never take Judge's place. "We had an amazing partnership," he says. "He was my best friend." ★

Policemen pay respects to a fellow officer as Judge takes his final walk to the hospital.

Roxy

FROM PET TO PARTNER

Pit bull ▪ New York

★ ★ ★ ★ ★ ★ ★ ★ ★ ★ ★ ★ ★

Walking onto the field at MetLife Stadium in front of thousands of people gathered for a New York Giants football game would give anyone stage fright. For a former marine affected by PTSD and wary of crowds, it's hell.

That can change, though, when you're there to present a service dog that you have trained for another similarly afflicted marine veteran. Amanda Donald admits that she feared she would pass out as she walked toward Frank Giaramida holding the leash of Scarlett, a German shepherd she had spent the past five months teaching to be Giaramida's companion. But she stayed focused on the veteran and Scarlett. "Everything else disappeared," Donald remembers of that moment. "I thought,

Scarlett is going to change someone's life the way Roxy changed mine."

Donald, a motor transportation operator, had been back in the United States for two years after a tour in Afghanistan before she realized the extent of her PTSD. Married to a fellow former marine and a mother of two young children, she had returned to college, but her anxiety levels became too high to continue. She struggled to sit through class. The VA hospital near her home in Long Island, New York,

OPPOSITE: *Earning service dog certification via Paws of War's training classes, Roxy helps her owner cope with PTSD.*

PIT BULL

- **Origin:** The first pit bull breeders envisioned a dog that combined the mettle of a bulldog with a terrier's spirit and agility.
- **Appearance:** Breeding prioritized function in the form: strong, compact bodies rather than pure looks.
- **Temperament:** Exuberant, good-natured, and sensitive
- **Training Tip:** Energetic social butterflies that love children, pit bulls aren't usually companionable with other dogs.

referred her to Paws of War, an organization that rescues dogs from shelters and trains them, free of charge, for veterans in need.

Donald called to ask if she could have one of her family's four pit bulls certified. The Paws of War trainers told her to bring a dog to class, and within a year, Donald's rescued dog Roxy had passed the service test. "It's like we share a brain and a heart," Donald says of her connection with Roxy. "She's changed everything. I used to feel like all eyes were on me when I would go out, but now they're looking at Roxy and talking about how beautiful she is."

Donald was not only able to return to college with Roxy by her side, but she also flourished. Far from white-knuckling her way through, Donald enjoys giving presentations now that she has Roxy—perpetually the most popular girl in class—standing in the front of the room with her.

Donald's husband, who also suffers from PTSD, was so inspired by the transformation he saw in his wife that he trained his rescued pit bull, Axle, to become his service dog. Shortly thereafter, the two agreed to begin training dogs for other veterans in need through Paws of War. They started with Molly, a rescued pit bull they trained for a veteran in a wheelchair. Then came Scarlett, the German shepherd who arrived at their house as an 11-week-old puppy. Scarlett and Donald quickly bonded. The night before giving her to Giaramida, Donald dreamed she had given away a daughter named Scarlett. She laughs telling the story, surprised by the depth of her attachment.

Donald remembers people at the game expressing concern about how difficult it would be to hand the leash over and find herself without the comfort of a dog. "I think I'll be OK," she responded, thinking of her four 90-pound pit bulls at home. Because of one in particular, it turns out, she's thriving. ★

Pit bulls are a treasured part of the Donald family, who now help train service dogs for other veterans in need.

Diamond

ALONG FOR THE RIDE

Labrador retriever mix ■ South Carolina

★ ★ ★ ★ ★ ★ ★ ★ ★ ★ ★ ★ ★

Technical Sergeant David Peacock enjoyed trips to Disney World before his deployments—of which there have been 12 in his 21-year career as a combat flight medic in the U.S. Army. He grew up near the amusement park and loved the rides as well as taking in the happy scene—a reminder, he says, of the lives for which he would risk his own.

But in 2006, Peacock was hurt in Afghanistan, hitting his head during a search-and-rescue mission. When he returned home to his wife and son in Columbia, South Carolina, he was so stricken with anxiety and depression that he was unable to leave his house.

Five years later, Peacock's wife, Virginia, called trainer Rick Kaplan at Canine Angels, a charity that rescues dogs from shelters and certifies them as service dogs for veterans. "I absolutely went behind Dave's back," laughs Virginia, a registered nurse. She has served as an Elizabeth Dole Foundation Fellow, helping raise awareness about the mental health care issues that veterans' caregivers and families face. "There are different times in our journey where our lives have changed," she says. "And this was one of them."

OPPOSITE: *Diamond bonded with veteran David Peacock before he even realized he needed her companionship.*

Peacock's resistance was, he admits, "denial, 100 percent. I thought I was fine." He says he was used to being the person who helps people, not the person who needed help. But when his wife asked him to be open-minded, he resolved to try.

Soon after, Peacock went to meet Kaplan and his intended partner, a Great Dane–Labrador mix named Blackjack. Aware that Peacock was suffering from dizzy spells and flashbacks, Kaplan chose a big dog on whom Peacock could lean his weight. "But Blackjack took one look at Peacock and walked the other way," Kaplan remembers. "Diamond, on the other hand, wouldn't leave him alone." Diamond's owners had surrendered him to the shelter for being too rambunctious, but in that room the strong Labrador retriever mix sold himself with his steadfast kindness, according to Kaplan.

> "How could you not love a dog who chooses you?"

Diamond continued to put his head in Peacock's lap while he talked with Kaplan, ignoring Kaplan's requests for him to go lie down. "How could you not love a dog who chooses you?" Peacock adds. "He somehow knew that I needed him."

With Diamond close, Peacock's panic attacks have subsided. He has enrolled in school and now enjoys, rather than avoids, trips to the mall and movies. There, watchful Diamond will raise his head to check on

FAVORITE PETS In 2016, Labrador retrievers celebrated their 25th consecutive year as the most popular dog in America, according to the American Kennel Club's registration stats. Labs have held the title longer than any breed in the AKC's 130-year-plus history, but poodles come in a close second after a 22-year leading streak in the early 1900s. Friendly, trainable Labs are terrific family pets that also readily perform as service dogs. German shepherds, golden retrievers, and beagles are also common pets, and the French bulldog is moving rapidly up the list.

Diamond has learned to love Disney World as much as her new family.

Peacock when there's a loud sound, but Peacock need only toss him a piece of popcorn to signal that everything's okay.

Most thrilling of all was the family's return to Disney World for the first time in years. Peacock braved many of the rides alongside Diamond, as service dogs are allowed on rides that don't require seat belts. Far from minding the crowds, Peacock also relished the attention paid to him and Diamond. "That's when I knew I was going to make it, that I would be OK," he says. "Since I got Diamond, I'm a different person. He's my buddy, my compadre." Not to mention, he's the perfect partner for a joy ride. ★

Animal behaviorist Kris Church-DiCiccio was having no luck in her search for a hearing dog to train for herself. Her first hearing dog was close to retirement age, but the efforts of local breeders and shelters had yet to turn up an heir. Then she and her husband got a call from a rescue organization trying to place an elkhound named Chara.

When asked if she could foster the dog, Church-DiCiccio recalls, "We just had this gut feeling that she was the *one*." Sure enough, that feeling was spot on. "She's the guardian angel who watches over us," Church-DiCiccio marvels.

Church-DiCiccio, who lives in Waynesboro, Virginia, and suffers from congenital hearing loss, quickly trained Chara to be her ears. A year later, an injury left Church-DiCiccio with dystonia, and she began to experience involuntary muscle contractions. Before Church-DiCiccio was even aware of an impending episode, Chara would block her from going anywhere. If she ignored Chara, the dog would paw her, bark, and go get someone else's attention. Soon, Chara was alerting Church-DiCiccio as long as 45 minutes before an episode, giving her ample time to take her medication and get to a safe place.

When Church-DiCiccio had her first baby, Chara also took him under her care. Two weeks after his birth, the baby stopped breathing one night. Chara awakened Church-DiCiccio, who was able to revive her son. Now the devoted pet patrols his bedroom, as well as that of his younger sibling.

Chara isn't always taking life so seriously. She enjoys playing with the other pets on the family farm, as well as hiking, hunting, and scavenging food scraps that the kids drop. "Of course she waits for the 'OK' signal from me," adds Church-DiCiccio. ★

Chara

LENDING AN EAR

Norwegian elkhound ▪ Virginia

OPPOSITE: *Chara, described as her family's "guardian angel," rests in a field of buttercups at the family farm.*

JJ

KEEPING WATCH OVER HER GIRL

Terrier mix ■ North Carolina

★ ★ ★ ★ ★ ★ ★ ★ ★ ★ ★ ★

Few bonds can compare to the profound love of a child and her dog. But imagine if that dog shares every moment of the child's life, not only as a playful companion, but also as her savior.

That is the relationship between KK Krawczyk and her terrier mix JJ, the first dog to be trained to detect the onset of a mastocytosis attack. A rare disease that results in allergic reactions to everything from stress to heat to illness, mastocytosis can cause quick anaphylaxis or fatal shock.

When KK turned four years old, her mother, Michelle Krawczyk, a nurse practitioner, realized that the sudden onset of KK's symptoms, which could occur several times a day, meant

that only she could monitor KK carefully enough. Kindergarten would be out of the question. Krawczyk was devastated.

"One night I was sitting with my husband talking about it," she remembers. "And our goofy goldendoodle, Nixon, sensing we were upset, laid his head on KK's dad's lap. He jokingly said to him, 'I wish you could go to school and look after her.'" Krawczyk laughed, "'Have you *met* Nixon?' We named him that because like the former president, he's not to be trusted."

OPPOSITE: *JJ accompanies seven-year-old KK Krawczyk into the operating room, where he will sit through her surgery.*

JJ attends her first day of school as a medical alert dog.

But she began to wonder if another dog might be better suited to the task.

Krawczyk hit dead ends with service dog providers for months before speaking with Deb Cunningham of Eyes Ears Nose and Paws in Carrboro, North Carolina, an organization that trains dogs to detect blood sugar level changes in people with diabetes. Cunningham asked Krawczyk if there might be a scent involved with KK's reactions; she couldn't make any promises, but Cunningham wanted to try to train a dog to help KK if the family was willing. Krawczyk called her husband and said, "She's nuts, but she's our only hope."

At the same time, Cunningham—who generally works with Labradors and retrievers—was training her first terrier mix. "I went to the shelter to pick up a golden retriever, but it had been adopted. A staff member stopped me and said, 'I think you might be interested in this terrier puppy.'" JJ turned out to be highly intelligent, and Cunningham's team quickly trained her as a diabetic assistance dog.

Shortly into JJ's training, Cunningham decided to test JJ and another terrier she was working with alongside three golden retrievers in the program, using a stopwatch to see how long it would take the dogs to detect a diabetes scent and alert the owner. The finding: The terriers needed only the time it took to get to the sample and then to her. The goldens, on the other hand, "would go in, say hello to everyone in the room, and then their noses would go up and they would alert. It was only an extra minute, but it was consistent."

Cunningham says terrier breeds have senses that are dialed to an 11 on a 1–10 scale. "You have a dog that's really alert, but you have to find a dog who is also flexible enough to learn to take in all the stimuli but remain alert." JJ had the rare ability to do both.

Ten months into JJ's 14-month-long training, Cunningham spoke with the Krawczyks and began to introduce the dog to the scent of mastocytosis using clothes that KK was wearing during an episode. Three months later, at an open house demonstrating the dogs' capabilities, JJ exhibited such strange behavior that Cunningham assumed she was sick. But as the crowds dispersed, JJ rushed over to KK—whom she had never met—and jumped on her. She then grabbed the emergency kit and brought it to KK's mother, who was also a stranger to her. Cunningham was stunned. "How did she know not to bring the kit to me or one of her other trainers?"

To Krawczyk this epitomizes JJ's extraordinary perception. "Her alert is a jump up and bark—we have trained her to be loud—but when we go to church, she will not bark. She grumbles, goes into my bag, and hands me my kit."

JJ is equally polite when the family is at the movies, but perhaps her most impressive public performance was accompanying KK into the operating room, thanks to the creativity of Duke University pediatric anesthesiologist Dr. Brad Taicher, who had worked with KK in the past. Knowing that KK can have a reaction to the anesthesia, Taicher spoke to her mother about having JJ in the room during a procedure that didn't require a completely sterile environment. The monitors would detect an irregularity, but Dr. Taicher believed JJ might do it earlier than the machines.

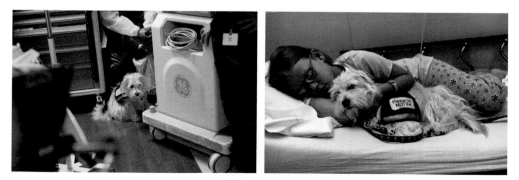

JJ monitors KK during surgery to preempt any adverse reactions to the anesthesia.

Cunningham brought JJ into the room, where she sat under a chair. A couple of times Cunningham would say, "JJ is acting up just a little bit," Taicher recalls, and while nothing appeared on the monitors, it correlated with what were increased times of stress with anesthesia. Taicher considers the experiment a success: "To have a stressed out little girl with mastocytosis is a potential disaster with anesthesia, and her being calm made our job easy. I'm sure having JJ with her both preoperatively and while she went to sleep helped us."

The comfort that JJ continues to provide KK's family is invaluable. KK was able to go to kindergarten part-time, with JJ by her side—making her the most popular girl in class. KK's mother sits in the back of the room should she need to administer medication, but KK no longer sleeps between her parents, who used to check on her every two hours to make sure she was still breathing.

"I don't have to set an alarm anymore because I know JJ will wake me up, as she has many times," says Krawczyk. "She's better than millions of dollars of equipment."

As for KK, her mother says her acceptance of the disease is in part thanks to her constant companion. "We talk about the good and the bad, and at times when she's in the hospital I'll say, 'I'm so sorry you're feeing bad,' and she'll say, 'It's OK, because I have Baby JJ, and I'm lucky because I get to take my best friend everywhere.'"

"We prayed for a miracle, and we got it," Krawczyk continues. "It didn't come in the form of modern medicine, but in a rescued pup dropped off at a shelter." ★

> "I'm lucky because I get to take my best friend everywhere."

SHOW TIME Tenacious terriers are suited to the celebrity lifestyle. Among the stars is a cairn terrier who played Toto in *The Wizard of Oz*, a rescued terrier who gained acclaim in the *Benji* franchise, and the beloved Jack Russell, Moose, from the TV sitcom *Frasier*.

Despite her serious job, JJ is still just a girl's best friend.

Mitchell

MAKING THE CASE FOR KINDNESS

Labrador retriever ■ Illinois

★ ★ ★ ★ ★ ★ ★ ★ ★ ★ ★ ★

Thanks to Mitchell, he and other dogs can have their day in court in Illinois. The yellow Labrador retriever, owned by the state's attorney's office, inspired the Illinois governor to pass a bill that allows trained facility dogs in courtrooms.

Mitchell was first assigned to the Lake County Children's Advocacy Center in 2015. A division of the state's attorney's office, the center and its 150-person staff assist in the investigation and prosecution of crimes involving sexual and physical abuse. In one year alone, it fielded 681 extreme cases of sexual abuse of children. For the victims, the families, and even those there to help, the emotional cost is brutal. Always looking for ways to reduce the stress level, state's attorney Michael Nerheim—a self-professed "dog guy"—attended a conference held by the Courthouse Dogs Foundation, a nonprofit organization started by a former Washington State prosecutor. Nerheim left convinced that a dog would be the solution.

Mitchell came to the department straight from Southwestern Illinois Correctional Center, where inmates spent almost two years training him as part of the Saint Louis–based nonprofit program called Support Dogs, Inc. "It's ironic given what he does now," grants

OPPOSITE: *Mitchell gives emotional support and encouragement to children who are victims of abuse.*

Mitchell's primary handler, Jason Grindel, the assistant state's attorney with whom the Labrador lives. "The warden fell so in love with Mitchell that he's kept in frequent touch with us."

Mitchell's prison training certified him as a service dog, able to perform such tricks as retrieving objects and opening and closing doors, including the refrigerator. But Grindel says he draws the line at some requests: "If I ask him to make the bed he looks at me as if he's saying, *'What?'*" Mitchell's job-specific commands include "visit" and "lap." Grindel explains that the former command tells Mitchell he can put his head on a child's thigh if she or he wants it, and the latter means that Mitchell can put his front paws over the child's lap. "He does it so delicately. It's so neat," Grindel adds.

Nerheim says Mitchell's affinity for contact and his ability to follow directions are crucial in these situations. "These kids have been abused repeatedly and often by a family member," he explains. "So they have experienced having no control in their lives. But Mitchell listens to them and obeys them." The retriever may also reduce the traumatic legal process by calming children during the interviews, which can be vital to the case: The better the interview, the stronger the case will be and less likely to go to trial.

Mitchell often soothes the adults, as well. The first day Mitchell was at the center, a mother and father came in with their daughter who had been abused. At first they weren't comfortable with their daughter being interviewed, but once they met Mitchell, Nerheim remembers, "They said, 'If he'll be there for our daughter, we are 100 percent in.'" Since that day, countless children in the center have fallen in love with a dog who distracts them from heinous circumstances.

Mitchell occasionally heads to the courthouse to roam the rooms of the specialty courts,

> "One day someone was crying in the front of the room, and Mitch was all the way in the back mingling. But when he heard her, he ran to her and sat at her feet. She just held on to him and sobbed."

Participants in the Walk With Mitchell fund-raiser gather. The event raised more than $3,000.

which include drug court, mental health court, and veterans' court. "He's so emotionally intelligent," Grindel says. "One day someone was crying in the front of the room, and Mitch was all the way in the back mingling. But when he heard her, he ran to her and sat at her feet. She just held on to him and sobbed."

Mitchell extends his reassuring presence with equal generosity to the staff members with whom he works every day. It's an invaluable service, particularly for a group that confronts unimaginable horrors. "Mitchell has been such a benefit to them," Nerheim says. "Even the grumpiest defense attorney, when he sees Mitchell in the hallway, gives him a hug, and the judges and lawyers have biscuits in their drawers for him. We just love him." Perhaps no one more than Grindel, who admits that he puts in extra hours as Mitchell's primary handler by day and chief tennis ball thrower by night. Hours, he says, that make him perhaps the only state employee who relishes overtime. ★

L eave it to a firefighter to recognize that when his Labrador retriever was lying down and rolling over, she was essentially doing a "Stop, drop, and roll." And so the Kasey Program was born, in which firefighter Jeff Owens and his two black Labs, both named Kasey, visit schools and teach children about fire safety.

The Kaseys—who live in Indianapolis, Indiana, but travel around the country—are a bit like Lassie: different dogs whose shared name has made them an icon to their young audience. Owens now teaches with the fifth- and sixth-generation Kaseys, search-and-rescue-trained service dogs who charm the children with their demonstrations. Among their tricks: how to crawl under smoke and check if a door is hot. The Kaseys are also the subject of songs that Owens, a theater major in college, sings to the students while he plays guitar. This trio teaches as many as 400,000 students a year.

"There's a natural affinity between children and dogs," says Owens, adding that the children greet the Kaseys enthusiastically by name even if

Kasey

UNFORGETTABLE FIREFIGHTER

Black Labrador ▪ Indiana

a year has passed between visits. That connection allows Owens to make an impression on students who might otherwise disengage. At one elementary school, Owens's discussion about smoke detectors inspired a brother and sister to ask their father to check those in their home. Finding that three of the five didn't work, he changed the batteries. Two weeks later, the family and their house were saved when the detectors went off during a fire. The credit, according to one of the children, went entirely to Kasey.

For Owens, there could be no greater praise. "Part of what drives me is I've pulled children out of houses, and I still live with those images," he says. "And I love what I'm doing. I get paid to play with my dog." ★

OPPOSITE: *Two Labrador retrievers who share the name Kasey have become the faces of fire safety for students.*

Xxon

LEADING THE WAY

German shepherd ▪ Texas

★ ★ ★ ★ ★ ★ ★ ★ ★ ★ ★ ★

When retired U.S. Air Force staff sergeant Michael Malarsie woke up in the hospital, his father had to tell him that the detonated IED in Afghanistan that blinded him had also killed four members of his team. Malarsie's immediate reaction was gratitude for his own relative good fortune. "I remember thinking, I have no right to feel sorry for myself," he says.

Two thoughts quickly followed: First, that Stevie Wonder is blind and always smiling, so it can't be terrible. And second: What do I need to be successful as a blind person? Malarsie knew he had to get a dog.

His caseworker introduced him to Fidelco Guide Dog Foundation, which trains German shepherds to be service dogs for the blind. After 10 months of rehabilitative therapy, during which Malarsie learned to navigate with a cane, he met three potential canine companions at the foundation's headquarters in Bloomfield, Connecticut. The first, a female, felt too small and active for Malarsie. The second, a male, was too big and goofy. Then out came Xxon (pronounced Exxon). "He walked in the room and he was just so stoic," Malarsie recalls. "I could feel it. He gave me a kiss and then lay

OPPOSITE: *Skillful guide dog Xxon shows his devotion by hanging close to his owner around the clock.*

The pair's relationship strengthened with time and eventually enabled Malarsie to return to work.

the few service dog foundations to send trainers to work with the dog and the handler on-site—cautioned patience. She explained to Malarsie that he and Xxon had to form a partnership, and that the bonding generally takes six months. "You're going to have trouble at the beginning," she warned. "It's not going to be easy."

Malarsie was thrilled not to be banging people in the ankles with a cane anymore, but the initial training of simply navigating the neighborhood was admittedly imperfect. "I'd get a phone call, get distracted, and more than once we'd end up lost, and I'd have to call Jesse on Skype so I could point my phone around and she could guide us home," Malarsie remembers. Jesse would have to determine Malarsie's location by identifying his surroundings through the video call.

It also took Malarsie time to adjust to Xxon's expression of devotion, which is not physical. Xxon sometimes dodged Malarsie's hand when he tried to pet him, and at first he took it personally. Now, Malarsie realizes that it's part of the shepherd's personality. "He doesn't like to be loved on," Malarsie continues. "He's not a black Lab getting in my face with kisses." But Xxon is deeply loyal, showing how much he cares in different ways. When Malarsie leaves a

down right next to me, ready to go to work."

Malarsie's wife, Jesse, was formerly married to one of the men who died in the explosion that blinded him, and Xxon arrived at their home in Texas on a significant day: "It was the one-year anniversary of my losing my sight and my wife losing her then husband, so you can imagine the mood in the house." But when their German shepherd showed up, "he changed everything," according to Malarsie.

Nevertheless, the adaptation to each other was slow. The caseworker from Fidelco—one of room, Xxon is a step behind, and he sticks by him 24 hours a day, seven days a week.

Xxon's gifts are certainly logistical: He is trained in useful commands as nuanced as "find the counter" at a hotel or store; "find the empty seat" in a waiting room; or "find inside" in a parking lot. But his companionship is equally valuable therapeutically. "It's difficult to return from combat, and a disability only compounds it," Malarsie explains. "If I didn't have Xxon, no one would talk to me. I could rob a bank, people are so uncomfortable talking to a blind person. But we can't go anywhere together without being approached by people who want to talk to us. He has made me feel like a part of society again."

> When Malarsie leaves a room, Xxon is a step behind, and he sticks by him 24 hours a day, seven days a week.

Thanks to the freedom and confidence that Xxon gave Malarsie to navigate the world, Malarsie was able to return to work in 2011, as well as to active duty status as the only blind airman serving in the U.S. Air Force at that time. He was recruited to helm a program that supports members of the Air Force who have been injured, and of the two-year experience, Malarsie says: "It was my chance not only to be of value to myself, but to show the Air Force I can still do a job even though I can't see."

The result is an even stronger bond with his dog and a feeling that anything is possible. Malarsie works with Xxon to help raise awareness about the wonders of service dogs—and his unforgettable companion in particular. ★

ALL EARS Dogs usually ignore speech and instead read body language—until they detect a familiar word such as "treat." Then a dog's ears will perk up and a head tilt positions one ear upward and forward facing the speaker for optimal listening. Some pups recognize our enthusiastic reactions to the adorable cocked head and use it for attention, although more often they're puzzling out the world.

Ralphie

A LESSON IN CARING

Shetland sheepdog mix ■ Virginia

★ ★ ★ ★ ★ ★ ★ ★ ★ ★ ★ ★ ★

As the star of the Shiloh Project, an organization dedicated to teaching compassion toward animals to at-risk youth, Ralphie gets more thank-you notes in a month than the average person receives in a lifetime. "Thank you. I learned there is hope for everybody," reads one letter addressed to the sheltie mix. Another begins, "Thank you for letting me pet you . . . I'm proud of you for being nice and not biting,"

Shiloh Project founder Nancy Katz Triplett rescued Ralphie, who has a special knack for giving back. The inspiring dog enters rooms of displaced, often depressed, teenagers and charms them into changing their minds about how animals should be treated. The program's goal is to make its young audience aware that animal violence and human cruelty are connected—and to help them understand that connection at a formative time in their lives. The first step is simple: ask the teens to get Ralphie to sit without touching him. "It's a revelation to them that you don't have to be physical to get a dog to do what you want it to," Triplett explains.

During his hour with these often transient teens, Ralphie is performing an equally

OPPOSITE: *The irresistible Ralphie was rescued from a shelter before he became a classroom superstar.*

impressive unstated trick: leading by example. Many of the teenagers identify with Ralphie's story of being abandoned in a shelter, where he sat overlooked, shy, and terrified. "It blows their mind to see the dog he is now, so gentle and going to them for affection," says Triplett. "I remind them that there are a lot of people who aren't seeing *their* potential, but they just need to get out of where they are now."

Triplett met Ralphie when a canine they had been using for the program passed away. She had called a shelter in Georgia looking for a quiet, calm dog suitable for the teenagers in the program, many of whom are afraid of dogs. The shelter workers picked Ralphie. Triplett had no intention of Ralphie becoming *her* dog, but the first night he was in foster care with another home, Triplett got a call to pick him up because the foster's dog wasn't a fan. "He walked up to me, curled up in my lap, and I said, 'Done!'" remembers Triplett, who lives with Ralphie in Fairfax, Virginia.

In addition to his gentle disposition, intelligence is one of Ralphie's greatest strengths. Triplett gives full training credit to the kids in her program, who have taught him how to give paw and crawl. "I do no work with him at home," Triplett admits with a laugh.

In the classroom, Ralphie responds to the attention by crawling into laps, a gift for teenagers often deprived of loving physical contact. He also wins hearts with his plea for a good belly rub, which he requests by rolling over and exposing his stomach. Triplett describes such an act of trust as magical for the teenagers. Thanks to the dog Ralphie has become, it's perfectly commonplace for him. ★

PART OF THE PACK Canines' natural affinity for children is thanks to their strong sense of social structure. In the wild, dogs vie for positions of leadership, but domesticated pets are part of a more straightforward hierarchy: The adults who feed them and set the rules are viewed as pack leaders, while young children are seen as fellow pack members who merit affection and protection. Though dogs have an instinct for knowing family, many are protective of kids even outside of their pack. Gentle and obedient breeds such as beagles, Irish setters, and Newfoundlands are known to be especially kid friendly.

Ralphie's easy presence eases the nerves of teens who might otherwise be afraid of dogs.

An old proverb says, "Good fences make good neighbors." Clearly, its author never had a neighbor like Andy, a golden retriever trained as a certified therapy dog. On a frigid February night in Chesterton, Indiana, Andy's routine walk would prove fateful.

Andy was let out into the yard with his housemates, two German shepherds and another golden retriever. "It was pitch dark, and something like 22 degrees with the wind chill," his owner, Vicki VanDenburgh, describes. Suddenly she heard Andy barking—a noisier, more excited bark than usual—and realized he had jumped the four-foot fence. VanDenburgh called out for him repeatedly, but Andy didn't respond.

When she went searching, she found Andy lying beside their elderly neighbor Starlene Hord, who had fallen in the snow as she got out of her car and trapped her right leg. "How did Andy know to come and get me?" Hord wonders. "He just stayed with me. It was like he was on a mission." When VanDenburgh was unable to lift Hord, Andy stood by her while VanDenburgh went to get her husband to help.

A trained service and therapy dog, Andy is accustomed to caring for the elderly thanks to weekly trips to Franciscan Saint Anthony Hospital in Michigan City, which have made him a beloved name throughout the community. He visits with everyone, but VanDenburgh observes that he has a special sense for finding the people who need him most. "He was born to do this," she marvels. "There are no words to express how naturally it comes to him."

What is instinct for Andy was lifesaving for Hord. "I would have died 10 feet from my house without him," she says. "He's my hero." ★

Andy

TO THE RESCUE

Golden retriever ■ Indiana

OPPOSITE: *A born hero, Andy seems to have a special intuition for knowing when someone needs help.*

Niko

CHANGING LIVES BEHIND BARS

Pit bull–corgi mix ■ Georgia

★ ★ ★ ★ ★ ★ ★ ★ ★ ★ ★

Mario Barber and his 11 fellow inmates didn't know what to expect when they prepared to meet the dogs with whom they would be living for the next nine weeks. Their soon-to-be cohabitants at Atlanta's Fulton County Jail were part of a pilot program called Canine CellMates, which rescues dogs from shelters and pairs them with inmates who are tasked with transforming the pets into well-behaved companions ready for adoption.

"It was crazy, because dogs in the jail—we never thought would happen," Barber remembers. The men stood in front of their bunks waiting to meet their canine assignments, each of them, says Barber, "wanting to be macho, paired with a pit bull or a rottweiler. And in walks my dog, little Niko," a laughing Barber recalls of the 35-pound pit bull and corgi mix.

"But it was all hugs and licks. And then it was nothing but love."

As founder and executive director Susan Jacobs-Meadows envisioned, Canine Cell-Mates saves dogs from the euthanasia list at shelters and turns them over to the incarcerated men who become, in her words, "the instruments of change." Jacobs-Meadows calls it an

OPPOSITE: *Thanks to the Canine CellMates program, Niko was rescued from a shelter and matched with a friend.*

opportunity to give back, particularly for men who carry guilt or shame for whatever reason they're in jail. "When that dog looks in their eye and trusts them—*wow,*" Jacobs-Meadows describes. "The goal is to change the hearts and minds of the inmates who come into the program, and then help them live different lives when they leave." To Jacobs-Meadows, the dogs—all of whom must pass the American Kennel Club Canine Good Citizen test—are therapy dogs first and foremost to their incarcerated trainers.

For the inmates, change begins the first day they meet the dogs and are introduced to the concept of positive reinforcement training. Jacobs-Meadows explains that many of the men grew up with dogs who were kept chained outside, and any kind of "training" involved intimidation and force. "The concept that you can change behavior without those things is pretty amazing to them," she says.

"At first, I'll be honest with you, I thought Miss Susan was crazy," Barber says. He couldn't imagine how they would teach the dogs to sit, lie down, and stay with hand signals—all in exchange for rewards offered from a treat pouch. But after working daily alongside volunteer trainers and pouring over the training handbook, Barber says he quickly saw the power of the approach. "Once we got started, it was a breeze. People think you have to use shock collars or be an alpha male, but you don't have to go through all that. I really didn't believe it, but the positive training is so wonderful."

Barber soon taught Niko not only basic commands, but also fancier tricks such as how to fetch his shower slippers. Niko slept by his bed at night, although Barber would have gladly shared his mattress: "He could have slept with me, but I'm big, and the beds are so small . . . I worried I would squish him." During the day, Niko would get in the bed and Barber would wrap him in blankets. "He was with me, every day, all of the time."

Nine weeks later, Niko, with Barber by his side, passed his Canine Good Citizen test.

> "The goal is to change the hearts and minds of the inmates who come into the program, and then help them live different lives when they leave."

With mutual respect and affection, Niko and Barber find ways to have fun in training class.

Niko's adoptive family, whom he joined after completing training, calls him Cookie.

Shortly thereafter, Niko met his new family: Jennifer Heckert and her young son. Heckert, an educator in California, had been through a rough divorce and wanted to get her son, an only child, a rescue dog to be his everyday companion. "The minute I met Niko, I thought it was destiny."

Heckert and her son went to the jail for Niko's graduation ceremony and spent a few hours with Barber. Heckert remembers, "He wanted to give me tips about the dog, and I could tell how attached he was to Niko, and how attached Niko was to Mario. It was very emotional. Mario cried, and Susan cried, too."

Barber vividly recalls the moment he handed Niko, now renamed Cookie, to his new family. "It was a tearjerker, and it hurt me giving him up. But when I saw the look on the face of the little boy he was going to, that made me happy." Barber would spend another year in jail, during which time he personally trained five dogs in addition to assisting the training of many others.

To those who think it's not a good thing to have the men give up their dogs and be heartbroken, Jacobs-Meadows says: "Life carries

GOOD BEHAVIOR Praise is the strongest dog training tool. Rewards, usually in the form of treats, and positive attention are the most effective way to teach commands. Timing is key, and the reward needs to come within seconds of seeing the desired behavior. Clickers are a good way to give rapid feedback and strengthen the connection between model behavior and reward.

with it unexpected happenings that involve tragedy and loss. And the lesson here is that if you keep doing the next right thing and making the next right decision, the next great joy is right around the corner." In the case of Canine CellMates, that joy is getting another dog and falling in love all over again.

Since being released, Barber has stayed an active member of Canine CellMates by attending events, helping with temperament assessments, and returning to the jail to speak with current members of the program. He credits the program with teaching him to love and even to be a better parent: "The dogs taught me it's about building a bond. You need to put in that time."

As a prisoner, Barber says his time with Niko gave him confidence he was lacking. "The dogs love you no matter what," he recognizes. "We can learn something from dogs, we really can." Those lessons are all the more poignant for the men given that they are training shelter dogs who are at risk for euthanasia. "For us to get a chance to save lives, to help them become blessings for someone else, I can't explain how powerful that is."

Heckert stays in touch, sharing stories and pictures of Cookie. "I look at those pictures and I cry," Barber admits. "But Niko's living a good life." For her part, Heckert intends to honor Barber's work with Cookie. "I have a dream that one day I'm going to remake him as a therapy dog," she says. "It has to come full circle, and we have to give back. This dog was put into the world for a reason." ★

Cookie shows young Heckert the same love and devotion he gave Barber.

Glory

A NOSE LIKE NO OTHER

Bloodhound ▪ California

★ ★ ★ ★ ★ ★ ★ ★ ★ ★ ★ ★

A canine or feline companion with a case of wanderlust—or simply a bad sense of direction—is no match for the nose and determination of Glory, a 130-pound bloodhound and real-life pet detective. Trained in search-and-rescue scent detection, Glory has assisted more than 1,800 cases in eight years on the job according to her owner and handler, Landa Coldiron.

Coldiron lives with Glory on a farm with dogs, horses, chickens, and cats in Sun Valley, California. She was inspired to search for lost pets more than a decade ago when she saw a segment on Animal Planet about Kat Albrecht, a former police officer who has made a career out of searching for and teaching others how to search for missing pets with the help of canine detective skills.

"I saw that and said, 'That's what I'm going to do for the rest of my life,'" remembers Coldiron, who signed up for search-and-rescue training. The capabilities of her teacher's bloodhound so impressed her that she soon began training her first bloodhound, Ellie May. Glory followed two years later.

Coldiron began working with Glory when she was eight weeks old. Training began with a

OPPOSITE: *Glory's gift for scent detection and directions has benefited local communities as well as her owner.*

BLOODHOUND

) **Origin:** Purity of pedigree and popularity among those of "noble blood" in England gave the bloodhound its name.

) **Temperament:** Bloodhounds are tireless trailers once they catch a scent, but despite their toughness, they are gentle and cuddly with family.

) **Training Tip:** Bloodhounds' wrinkled faces, loose-hanging skin, and sagging ears make a solemn expression, but they have high energy levels and should get plenty of playtime.

lesson that Coldiron calls "puppy runaway" during which a friend would hold Glory while she ran down a path with her rescued pit bull. When Glory followed and found them, she would be rewarded with food. Coldiron gradually increased the distance and the search duration, "aging" the trail by covering the scent and adding twists and turns. Within months, Glory was ready to search for animals that she had never met, given only the smell of their bedding to track.

Glory's many successes include a Pomeranian who escaped when her owners went into the hospital and a well-meaning neighbor took her to work in an industrial area 60 miles from home. After nine days of searching, the dog owner's daughter called Coldiron; Glory found the dog cowering under palettes of tile in a factory yard within three hours.

The bloodhound is also an ace at locating cats, although Coldiron says that when they are working in Southern California, most felines have met their fate at the hands of predators by the time she is asked to help. There is comfort nevertheless: "People call me when they want closure," she explains. "It's so much better to know than still be wondering, five years later."

Glory accompanies Coldiron everywhere, although her stubbornness can make traveling complicated. When she decided several years ago that she didn't like elevators, no amount of coaxing could convince her otherwise, so Coldiron now stays only on the ground floor of hotels.

But for all her obstinacy, Glory is devoted—with one caveat, explains Coldiron: "If I took her off the leash and she saw a rabbit or squirrel, I'd never see her again." Fortunately, this search-and-rescue star is staying on the path. ★

Glory sniffs around for traces of missing pets or people to help find their location.

Dino

Belgian Malinois ■ Texas

★ ★ ★ ★ ★ ★ ★ ★ ★ ★ ★ ★

Almost three years after the death of their son Marine Staff Sergeant Christopher Diaz, Sal and Sandra Diaz adopted a six-year-old Belgian Malinois named Dino. It was a homecoming of sorts for Dino: He had been Christopher Diaz's constant companion in Afghanistan, where the two searched for explosive devices, and Dino was by Diaz's side when an explosive device killed him as he rushed to the aid of a fellow marine.

The Diaz family waited three years to welcome Dino to their home in El Paso, Texas. They had spoken about the possibility of adopting him soon after Christopher's death, but they knew Dino couldn't replace their son, and the young dog had good work yet to do in the field. Sal remembers his wife saying that she didn't think Christopher would want them to adopt Dino while there were still some lives for him to save. So the couple wrote a letter saying that when the time came, they would like to be the first family considered to adopt the dog.

When Sandra and Sal first met the noble Belgian Malinois, Sal remembers with a laugh, "He didn't take kindly to me—he showed me

OPPOSITE: *Now a cherished member of the Diaz family, Dino stood by Marine Sergeant Christopher Diaz.*

BELGIAN MALINOIS

> **Origin:** All Belgian Malinois are descendants of two herding dogs named Vos I and Lise de Laeken, chosen for their stamina and smarts.

> **Temperament:** Belgian Malinois are good workers because they see every task as a game. They also make enthusiastic and loyal workout companions.

> **Appearance:** Easily mistaken for German shepherds, Belgian Malinois are smaller and more lithe.

his tush! But he went right up to my wife and put his head on her hands."

Dino has rare attributes: Born and trained in Israel, he can respond to commands in both Hebrew and English; he's a specialized search dog who can follow directions from a radio headset to sniff out bombs, weapons, and drugs. What wasn't part of his repertoire upon arriving in Texas after six years of marine service was acting like a pet. When Christopher's then eight-year-old son and nine-year-old daughter first met their father's former companion, they were told to be patient because the dog wasn't used to playing. In the military, Dino had minimal rest, and then it was "train, train, train," Sandra explains.

Still, Dino had no trouble making himself comfortable. When he walked through the door of his new home, his first move was to jump on the sofa with his chew toy. Sal recalls, "He was immediately happy. He knew it was his home." Soon Dino, whose rambunctiousness reminds the Diazes of their son, was romping freely. Sandra and Sal alternate playing outside with the high-energy dog, and both are delighted to meet his need for affection, which he isn't shy about requesting; when he wants to be pet, he walks up and taps them with his paw.

For the couple, bringing Dino into the family has allowed for unexpected joy. "With Dino, we have something Christopher loved and took care of 24/7," says Sal, who senses that Dino knows they are Chris's parents. Adds Sandra, "He was a part of my son, and knowing that when Chris passed away, Dino was the last thing he touched or petted is comforting to me." ★

The Diazes attended the Veterans Parade in New York, where Christopher and Dino were honored for their service.

Kai

AN EYE ON THE BALL

Labrador retriever ■ Texas

★ ★ ★ ★ ★ ★ ★ ★ ★ ★ ★

Forget dalmatians: In San Antonio, Texas, a firefighter's best friend is a Labrador retriever, specifically a former shelter dog named Kai. Trained as an accelerant detector, Kai has worked more than 200 fire and bomb investigations with her handler Justin Davis, who began the city's K-9 program in 2010.

One of Kai's most memorable discoveries took her only a moment but won her a Hero Dog Award from the American Humane Association. When a two-alarm fire broke out in a mall—collapsing the ceiling and creating tons of debris—Kai detected a melted gasoline container under the rubble within eight seconds. The find helped the state prove that the fire was intentionally set. Davis calls Kai the best tool available. "I've never seen her scared of anything. When she's working, she's like a machine."

Kai's talent wasn't discovered in an elite training program, but rather in a shelter, where an observant employee noticed that when Kai dove into a pile of toys she would retrieve only the tennis ball. Impressed by her nose and drive, and charmed by her sweet personality, the visitor got in touch with a Humane Society board member; she in turn

OPPOSITE: *Ace accelerant detector Kai is one of dozens of dogs that support San Antonio's K-9 program.*

called State Farm, a scholarship provider for Davis's then nascent program. The company agreed to train Kai, saving her from euthanasia at the shelter.

Months later, Kai was introduced to Davis. "When I first met her, I thought she was nuts," Davis admits. "I was expecting a dog where you say 'down' and they're down." But once Davis understood Kai's obsessive desire to retrieve, the pair clicked. "She will literally retrieve until she drops dead if you don't stop her," he says. "She has 'stop' and 'go,' and nothing in between."

The result is a dog who likes to slumber on her special love seat in the evening but jumps up every morning, eager to be back on duty. Davis compares working with the ever energetic Kai to holding on to lightning.

"I understand we are paired up with dogs who are like us, and I'm not sure what that means about me," laughs Davis, a man who considers it relaxing to teach a boot camp exercise class in his free time. Kai's reward for working hard all day is heading to the backyard and playing fetch with Davis, who admits he throws the ball "a *lot.*"

In addition to games of fetch, mealtimes are devised to cement their connection. Kai receives 100 percent of her nutrition out of Davis's hand—save the table scraps she coerces from his wife. "When you're talking about providing every single meal a day, every day, plus more food as rewards, it's hard not to have a bond," says Davis. Especially when the hand that feeds is rewarded with kisses. ★

WOOF TRANSLATION Not all barks are created equal, according to research. Spectrograms, or pictures, of barks from the same dog reveal that the sound can vary in timing, pitch, and amplitude. The question is if the various barks convey different meaning. Researchers have recorded "food growls" as well as "stranger barks" and "alone barks" to experiment with other dogs' and humans' perceptions of the vocalizations. The finding: Most people—whether dog owners or not—could tell just from hearing the bark if a dog was alone or if a stranger was approaching, or if the dog was playful or aggressive. People could also distinguish between dogs by their stranger barks.

The spirited Kai and her partner work seamlessly together investigating potential arson cases.

Xander had a rough start in life: As a puppy, the pug lost his eyes in an accident and was surrendered to a shelter in Klamath Falls, Oregon. But then an adoption set him on a new course.

The Beedy family, which includes eight other pugs and a Labrador retriever, welcomed Xander into their home without hesitation. Immediately, Rodney and Marcie Beedy enrolled Xander in obedience classes. Marcie wore an ankle bracelet with little bells on it so Xander would be audibly cued to heel, but Rodney says that's the only special assistance the dog has ever needed. "He jumps off the couch and flies out the doggie door, and he'll walk up to counters and move around them before he hits them," Rodney observes.

Xander's preternatural instinct is more than physical: His ability to read people's needs make him a gifted therapy dog. Honored by the American Kennel Club, Xander's talents are now used on behalf of Hands & Words Are Not For Hurting, for which he is an ambassador. The project asks students to take a 14-word pledge: "I will not use my hands or my words for hurting myself or others." Program founder and executive director Ann Kelly explains, "He visually brings the message loud and clear that it's not OK if someone hurts you or you hurt other people, and he's so joyful. I wish I had a million Xanders."

At home, Xander has taught himself to detect Marcie's diabetic episodes, waking her in the middle of the night when necessary. By day, he is so busy with Hands & Words and visiting hospitals and hospices that Rodney estimates Xander interacts with some 5,700 children a year. "He's at his most comfortable when he is in the middle of a crowd of 200 kids," says Rodney. ★

Xander

A LITTLE DOG WITH A BIG MESSAGE

Pug ■ Oregon

OPPOSITE: *Xander embraces petting hands and inspires smiles at Tiny Hopefuls Daycare.*

Resources

★ ★ ★ ★ ★ ★ ★ ★ ★ ★ ★ ★ ★

4 Paws for Ability
4pawsforability.org
937-374-0385
Info@4PawsForAbility.org

Animal Farm Foundation
animalfarmfoundation.org
845-868-7559
info@animalfarmfoundation.org

American Humane Association
americanhumane.org
800-227-4645
info@americanhumane.org

American Kennel Club
akc.org

Canine Angels
canineangelsusa.org
917-575-6235

Canine CellMates
caninecellmates.org

404-399-6392
info@caninecellmates.org

Charlotte's Litter
charlotteslitter.org

Conservation Canines
conservationbiology.uw.edu/conservation
   -canines
206-745-2460
CK9s@uw.edu

Courthouse Dogs Foundation
courthousedogs.com

Deja Foundation
www.dejafoundation.org
646-580-3352
info@dejafoundation.org

Eyes Ears Nose and Paws
eenp.org
919-408-7292
info@eenp.org

Fidelco Guide Dog Foundation
fidelco.org
860-243-5200
info@fidelco.org

Guiding Dogs for the Blind
guidingeyes.org

Hands & Words Are Not
for Hurting Project
handsproject.org
503-587-4853
info@handsproject.org

Heeling House
heelinghouse.org
571-409-1228

Humane Society of the United States
humanesociety.org
866-720-2676

Lutheran Church Charities
K-9 Comfort Dogs
lutheranchurchcharities.org
866-455-6466
info@k9comfort.org

National Disaster Search Dog Foundation
www.searchdogfoundation.org
888-459-4376
Rescue@SearchDogFoundation.org

Paws Humane
pawshumane.org
706-565-0035
adopt@pawshumane.org

Paws of War
pawsofwar.org
631-406-6595
info@PawsOfWar.org

Pets Helping Agriculture in Rural
Missouri (PHARM Dog USA)
pharmdog.org
660-235-0128

Support Dogs
supportdogs.org
314-997-2325

The Shiloh Project
theshilohproject.org
shilohproject@me.com

Zeke Gear
zekegear.com

Canine Good Citizen® Training & Testing

BY THE AMERICAN KENNEL CLUB

★ ★ ★ ★ ★ ★ ★ ★ ★ ★ ★ ★

Before taking the Canine Good Citizen test, owners will agree to the Responsible Dog Owners Pledge that affirms their commitment to taking care of their dogs' health needs, safety, exercise, training, and quality of life. Owners also agree to show responsibility by performing such duties as cleaning up after their dogs in public places and never letting dogs infringe on the rights of others. Once the pledge is completed, owners and their dogs are ready to start the test:

TEST 1: Accepting a Friendly Stranger

This test demonstrates that the dog will allow a friendly stranger to approach it and speak to the handler in a natural, everyday situation. The evaluator walks up to the dog and handler and greets the handler in a friendly manner, ignoring the dog. The evaluator and handler shake hands and exchange pleasantries. The dog must show no sign of resentment or shyness.

TEST 2: Sitting Politely for Petting

This test demonstrates that the dog will allow a friendly stranger to touch it while it is out with its handler. With the dog sitting at the handler's side, to begin the exercise, the evaluator pets the dog on the head and body. The handler may talk to his or her dog throughout the exercise. The dog may stand in place as it is petted. The dog must not show shyness or resentment.

TEST 3: Appearance and Grooming

This practical test demonstrates that the dog will welcome being groomed and examined and will permit someone, such as a veterinarian, groomer, or friend of the owner, to do so. It also demonstrates the owner's care, concern, and sense of responsibility. The evaluator inspects the dog to determine if it is clean and groomed. The dog must appear to be in healthy condition (i.e., proper weight, clean, healthy, and alert).

TEST 4: Out for a Walk (Walking on a Loose Lead)

This test demonstrates that the handler is in control of the dog. The dog may be on either side of the handler. The dog's position should leave no doubt that the dog is attentive to the handler and is responding to the handler's movements and changes of direction. The dog need not be perfectly aligned with the handler and need not sit when the handler stops.

TEST 5: Walking Through a Crowd

This test demonstrates that the dog can move about politely in pedestrian traffic and is under control in public places. The dog and handler walk around and pass close to several people (at least three). The dog may show some interest in the strangers but should continue to walk with the handler, without evidence of over-exuberance, shyness, or resentment. The handler may talk to the dog and encourage or praise the dog throughout the test. The dog should not jump on people in the crowd or strain on the leash.

TEST 6: "Sit" and "Down" on Command and Staying in Place

This test demonstrates that the dog has training, will respond to the handler's commands to sit and down, and will remain in the place commanded by the handler (sit or down position, whichever the handler prefers). The dog must do "sit" and "down" on command, and then the owner chooses the position for leaving the dog in the stay.

TEST 7: Coming When Called

This test demonstrates that the dog will come when called by the handler. The handler will walk 10 feet from the dog, turn to face the dog, and call the dog. The handler may use encouragement to get the dog to come. Handlers may choose to tell dogs to "stay" or "wait," or they may simply walk away, giving no instructions to the dog.

TEST 8: Reaction to Another Dog

This test demonstrates that the dog can behave politely around other dogs. Two handlers and their dogs approach each other from a distance of about 20 feet, stop, shake hands, exchange pleasantries, and continue on for about 10 feet. The dogs should show no more than casual interest in each other. Neither dog should go to the other dog or its handler.

TEST 9: Reaction to Distraction

This test demonstrates that the dog is confident at all times when faced with common distracting situations. The evaluator will select and present two distractions. Examples of distractions include dropping a chair, rolling a crate dolly past the dog, having a jogger run in front of the dog, or dropping a crutch or cane. The dog may express natural interest and curiosity and/or may appear slightly startled but should not panic, try to run away, show aggressiveness, or bark.

TEST 10: Supervised Separation

This test demonstrates that a dog can be left with a trusted person, if necessary, and will maintain training and good manners. Evaluators are encouraged to say something like, "Would you like me to watch your dog?" and then take hold of the dog's leash. The owner will go out of sight for three minutes. The dog does not have to stay in position but should not continually bark, whine, or pace unnecessarily, or show anything stronger than mild agitation or nervousness.

Note: This does not include the complete requirements. See akc.org/dog-owners/training /canine-good-citizen for more information about the Canine Good Citizen test.

Illustrations Credits

★ ★ ★ ★ ★ ★ ★ ★ ★ ★ ★ ★

95, Chris Sweetwood; 96, Julie Howery; 99, Lori M. Nichols/South Jersey Times; 100, Courtesy of Amanda Donald; 103 (LE), Courtesy of Amanda Donald; 103 (UP RT), Dori Scofield, Courtesy of Paws of War; 103 (LO RT), Courtesy of Amanda Donald; 104, Courtesy of Virginia Peacock; 107 (BOTH), Courtesy of Virginia Peacock; 108, Chris Church-DiCiccio; 110, Shawn Rocco/Duke Health; 112, Maria Ikenberry, courtesy of Eyes, Ears, Nose, and Paws; 113 (LE), Shawn Rocco/Duke Health; 113 (RT), Michelle Krawczyk; 115, Morgan Brough Photography, courtesy of Michelle Krawczyk; 116, Lake County State's Attorney's Office staff member; 119, Jackie Borchew and the Deerfield Rotary Club; 120, Jeff Owens, courtesy of Kasey Program; 122, Jesse Malarsie; 124, Jesse Malarsie; 126, Courtesy of the Shiloh Project; 129, Courtesy of the Shiloh Project; 130, Courtesy of Vicky VanDenburgh; 132, Amy Jackson/Karmalized Pictures; 135 (UP LE), Dan Jacobs/DVJ Images, courtesy of Canine CellMates; 135 (UP RT), Courtesy of Canine CellMates; 135 (LO), Amy Jackson/Karmalized Pictures; 136, Jennifer Heckert; 137, Jennifer Heckert; 138, Courtesy of Landa Coldiron; 141, Courtesy of Landa Coldiron; 142, Courtesy of Sal and Sandra Diaz; 145, Courtesy of Sal and Sandra Diaz; 146, Albert Pedroza/SAFD; 149, Helen L. Montoya/San Antonio Express-News/ZUMA Press; 150, Steven Silton/Herald and News.

Since 1888, the National Geographic Society has funded more than 12,000 research, exploration, and preservation projects around the world. National Geographic Partners distributes a portion of the funds it receives from your purchase to National Geographic Society to support programs including the conservation of animals and their habitats.

National Geographic Partners
1145 17th Street NW
Washington, DC 20036-4688 USA

Become a member of National Geographic and activate your benefits today
at natgeo.com/jointoday.

For information about special discounts for bulk purchases, please contact
National Geographic Books Special Sales: specialsales@natgeo.com

For rights or permissions inquiries, please contact National Geographic Books
Subsidiary Rights: bookrights@natgeo.com

ISBN: 978-1-4262-1773-9

Printed in China

16/RRDS/1

A Unique
BND

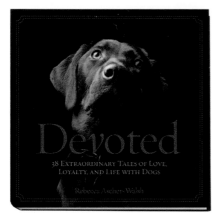

Celebrate extraordinary tales of love in these heartwarming collections of portraits and stories about people and the special bond they share with their dogs. Uplifting, inspiring, and filled with unforgettable images, these books are perfect for anyone who cherishes man's best friend.